The Complete

IDIOT'S

Guide to

VCRs

by Jim Holt with
Tershia d'Elqin

alpha
books

A Division of Prentice Hall Computer Publishing

11711 North College Avenue, Carmel, Indiana 46032 USA

International Standard Book Number:1-56761-294-6
Library of Congress Catalog Card Number: 93-72007

95 94 93   9 8 7 6 5 4 3 2 1

Interpretation of the printing code: the rightmost number of the first series of numbers is the year of the book's printing; the rightmost number of the second series of numbers is the number of the book's printing. For example, a printing code of 93-1 shows that the first printing of the book occurred in 1993.

Screen reproductions in this book were created by means of the program Collage Plus from Inner Media, Inc., Hollis, NH.

Printed in the United States of America

Publisher, Marie Butler-Knight; **Associate Publisher**, Lisa A. Bucki; **Managing Editor**, Elizabeth Keaffaber; **Development Editor**, Seta Frantz, **Manuscript Editor**, Howard Pierce; **Cover Designer**, Jean Bisesi; **Designer**, BarbWebster; **Indexer**, Craig A. Small, **Production Team**; Diana Bigham, Katy Bodenmiller, Brad Chinn, Scott Cook, Tim Cox, Meshell Dinn, Terri Edwards, Mark Enochs, Howard Jones, Wendy Ott, Ryan Rader, Beth Rago, Carrie Roth, Marc Shecter, Greg Simsic

Special thanks to Ed Palpant for ensuring the technical accuracy of this book.

Trademarks

Contents

Introduction

A VCR is Not Just Another Way to Tell Time!

Does it faze you to hear words like "VHF/UHF" or "RF cable"? Do your eyes glaze over while you stare uncompre-hendingly at the mumbo jumbo in your manuals? Okay, you're really no idiot.  But face it, you still have problems untangling the mess of cables which feed your home entertainment system. Relax; everyone does.

People flock to plunk down several hundred dollars for a VCR. But those who can fully operate these expensive machines are the exception rather than the rule. While almost everyone can extract an audio-visual from a rented movie, preprogramming a VCR to record a broadcast show usually has all the reliability of a crap shoot.

The instructions packaged with your VCR, television, stereo and cable box may as well have come from the moon. They may have been crudely translated from Japanese or German. At best, they were written by someone with a nose for electronics but not a clue about English.

Perhaps you purchased your components one at a time, little thinking that to put the whole thing together would be like wiring Elm Street for your own personal nightmare.

If matching the VCR instructions to sundry wires and gizmos makes you feel like sticking your fingers in a socket, this book is for you. Your VCR will virtually become the brains behind your entire entertainment system. With this book you will learn how to:

☞ Coordinate your movies, antenna, and cable through your VCR.

☞ Clean and maintain your VCR for better and longer VCR life.

☞ Tape one show while watching another.

☞ Save money on the cable hook-ups inside your house.

☛   Plug into cable radio free.

☛   Use your camcorder and VCR to create family photo albums.

☛   Spend your money wisely on new set-ups.

In short, this book will more than pay for itself.

It doesn't take a genius to get the most out of an entertainment system; it takes only a little time and willingness to "plug in, plug out, and play."

How I Got into Video Consulting

Believe it or not, I've actually been called to over 9,000 homes and innumerable companies in which people were at loggerheads with their VCRs. The problems were often simple, but they were having problems nevertheless.

My career as a video consultant started unintentionally. I was a professional announcer doing voice-overs for radio, TV and creating special commercials for some of my clients. One of my customers owned a video business. I did a series of commercials for his company on radio and TV, writing, producing, and actually acting in them at times.

One day, this generous man asked whether I would go over and see one of his friends who was having a terrible time with his VCR. The guy was at the point of heaving his machine out the window. Since he had the same cable company as I, he let me play around with his set.

So, just like the proverbial snowball, the business grew, first to include his friends that found out that cable wouldn't preclude VCR operation, then people they knew with antenna problems and so forth.

I ran a small inexpensive ad which brought in about twenty calls. I was unsure of myself and admitted it. But these people still seemed to welcome me. They were desperate. We managed to struggle through and figure out what was wrong.

As one appointment led to another, I learned more and more until I developed proficiency about eleven years ago. I put the work I had been doing in the radio, television, and acting business aside to make video consulting a full-time occupation.

How This Book Came to Be

I've derived a lot of personal joy from my home electronics system and I've experienced a vicarious pleasure from helping others get their systems in shape. It's great to hear people say, "Hey, there's nothing to this. It's not that frustrating after all."

While I can help people in my area personally, I thought a simple book might alleviate the anxiety level in far-flung places like Detroit and Dubuque. So I've reworked a few of the notes I've kept over the last years, and this book is the result.

You will find that I repeat important information throughout the book, especially in tips. I feel that repetition works very well in teaching people how to properly operate and maintain their VCRs. Sometimes that first run through just goes in one ear and out the other of the person listening (or half-listening). This isn't uncommon for subjects that are outside a person's usual understanding. A little extra emphasis here and there is in this book, and if you see it repeating on occasion, you'll know why. Here's an example tip.

> ## Tip
>
> **Don't Forget!**   Remember to put the VCR on channel 3.

A Sony TV bought yesterday will obviously be different from a Panasonic bought twenty years ago. You may need to dig out your manual if your TV is labeled with names that differ from those I'm using, or if the knob on the left looks like the one I describe as the knob on the right. The same goes for different brands (and vintages) of VCRs. The front panel on your VCR may have more buttons than the bridge of the starship Enterprise, but don't worry, it's all decipherable.

Oh, by the way, during my past 10 years of video consulting, some amusing, somewhat strange, and often very exciting things have happened. To let you know that you're not the only baffled VCR user out there, I'll share a few stories with you. You'll find out that even brain surgeons have a hard time programming their VCR.

A VCR History Lesson

I am often asked, "What happened to Beta?" So I did a little research and came up with a few conflicting stories. The one I hear most is this:

Professional commercial videotape machines were first demonstrated as far back as 1956 by Ampex, and home video recorders appeared on retail shelves in early 1976. Sony gave birth to the Beta VCR when their engineering efforts turned the reel-to-reel video tape into the video cassette. Beta served the consumer well. Just about everyone seemed satisfied with what was happening at that time.

Suddenly, as is so often the case in technology, something new and slightly different took video viewing by storm.

As the story goes, VHS (video home system) was actually developed by a Sony engineer. He took his invention to the top dogs at Sony. Although VHS showed advantages over Beta, for whatever reasons, the dogs didn't snap up his idea. The gentleman was then free to move forward to make a presentation to the Matsushita company.

The inventor spoke with the higher echelons at Matsushita, explaining VHS's edge over Beta. When the tape is stopped, rewound, or fast-forwarded or reversed, it leaves the head. It provides longer life to the tape and to the heads. Other advantages, such as a lighter machine, were also promoted.

Well, Matsushita saw great promise in all this and made a fantastic offer which the inventor quickly accepted. They then took the VHS system right to the top. It wasn't long before VHS surpassed the Beta system.

Matsushita is a huge company, which now produces video players and VCRs in Japan for world export. The company takes up several city blocks.

It took a few years for Sony to recover from that blow. Everyone now uses the VHS system (including Sony!). The Beta system at this writing is used only by Sony, on a very expensive machine.

What to do about all that existing Beta footage? Although one can save footage by having a copy made from a Beta VCR to a VHS VCR, there is some quality loss. But if it's important footage to the owner, that's what counts.

The home-video viewing evolution continues. New developments include high-definition television (HDTV) with additional lines of resolution that constitute increased clarity and diversification. The future of optics is limitless. What's next—holographs? Maybe.

Lesson 1

Okay, I've Got It Plugged In— Now What?

Although trying to work VCRs into a media system all too often turns normal folks into raving lunatics, VCRs seem in and of themselves pretty straightforward. All VCRs (except camcorders) fit neatly on a table and use a power outlet for electricity. Most people have no problem plugging them in and finding the power switch. They all have a loading mechanism and the requisite buttons—Play, Stop, Pause, Record, Fast Forward, Rewind, and Eject. Even though there are many different manufacturers and some VCRs are clunkier than others, these features remain constant and pretty much self-explanatory.

On the back of your VCR are the input/output terminals—little holes that enable you to marry the VCR to your other electronics. Here is your first challenge: How do you match all these little holes with all the holes on the back of all your other machines? Now, easy does it. Just read along, following whatever applies to your circumstances. This book will make those several hundred dollars you plopped down for your

VCR well worth it. If you are in the market for a new VCR, however, the section at the end of this lesson looks at some features you should consider when making your purchase.

Catch a Wave—Determining How You Receive Television Signals

Before hooking up your VCR to the TV, you must know what kind of reception you have. An isolated few have no reception; these people have purchased VCRs merely to watch existing cassette tapes, like every Clint Eastwood western ever made or the complete Alfred Hitchcock oeuvre. But most of us receive television signals via cable, antenna, or satellite.

Tip

Recorder or Player? If you bought a VCR just for playing movies, I suggest you pack it up and return it immediately. Then buy a video player, which has about half the parts and costs about half as much.

Cable

A cable TV signal is sent to subscribers for a monthly fee by means of a cable. The signal comes into your house on a single, insulated coaxial cable. Cable subscribers receive from 2 to over 60 channels. Some channels—such as HBO, Showtime, and Disney—are scrambled when they reach your house; they are unscrambled when you pay your cable company an additional monthly fee. The channel numbers are different for cable subscribers than for those receiving signals by antenna and satellite because cable systems change them. Cable subscribers receive a list of all available cable channels and the corresponding channel numbers for those channels available by antenna.

Here are some advantages of cable reception:

- ☞ Cable offers clear reception of all channels without the need for an antenna and motor device.

- ☞ Cable reception offers more channels than antenna reception.

- ☞ Cable subscribers receive free service for correcting cable problems.

- ☞ Cable provides complete monthly cable listings through a cable guide at a small additional cost.

Antenna or Rabbit Ears

Either because they do not want to (or cannot) bear the cost of cable or because cable service is not available in their area, many people still rely on outdoor antennas or on indoor antennas, also called *rabbit ears*.

Satellite Dish

If you own a bar or you live in the sticks, you may have satellite reception. Or maybe you hanker for still more channels than supplied by cable. People with satellite reception know they have it, because owning a satellite dish is like owning an elephant.

Once you've determined which kind of reception you have, skip to one of the lessons which follow for detailed instructions on how to hook up your specific system.

The Gizmos You'll Need

You're not the electronics type. That's why you're reading this book. But listen up: Only a thin border actually separates all you so-called right-brained people from the left-brained wiring wizards. To cross that border, all you need is some basic information and a few special accessories.

The basic information is not nearly as complicated to acquire as the knack for creativity which you've cultivated instead of electronics efficiency. That's what the bulk of this book provides: basic information.

And accessories! Ever marvel at the speed with which someone with a ratchet wrench or power drill fixed something you'd been monkeying with unsuccessfully for hours . . . or days? Tools really do separate the men from the boys. They can also separate the women from the men who act like boys. In the case of VCRs, the tools are accessories. Accessories are the key to top-performing machinery.

Here are several accessories, available from your electronics store, for you to learn about and add to your vocabulary. They are used in a variety of ways throughout this book. If you don't learn about them here, you'll be stumped and apoplectic later. So take some time to familiarize yourself with the names and appearances of each. If you're the tactile type, take this book to an electronics store and ask the salesperson to plunk one of each in your paw so you can get the feel of them. They're hard. They're heavy. They have sharp corners. But don't worry. They won't hurt you and they're useful.

It happens every time: The back of the machine has a couple of screws, and the wire that's supposed to attach to it is round with a little pin in it. One of the greatest frustrations of electronics installation is incompatible holes and plugs, or *inputs* and *outputs*. Probably the single most magnificent thing about the following gizmos is their ability to help you make these incompatible connectors (called *finishes*) connect—to mate your machines.

☞ Round coaxial cable, which features a solid center conductor surrounded by a heavy plastic called the *dielectric* (see Figure 1.1). Around this is a mesh of braid that acts as a second conductor and a shield against external interference. The entire cable is insulated with black plastic. This type of cable is used by telephone companies, cable companies, and by you. It provides excellent reception because it is protected. It is called *coaxial* because has within it two *axes,* which accommodate both the VHF and UHF input bands. The cable you buy has two "male" ends (each with a needle). Sometimes it is called *RF cable*; RF stands for *R*adio *F*requency.

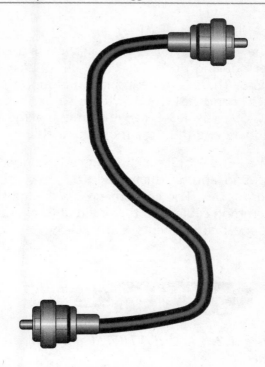

Figure 1.1.   *Round coaxial cable.*

☛ UHF/VHF/FM matching transformer. This is a flat wire, coated with plastic, with two separate wires ending in horse-shoe-shaped finishes (see Figure 1.2).

> ### Tip
>
> There are three types of coaxial cable used for hooking up VCRs: RG-59, RG-11, and RG-6. There is more insulation around the RG-11 and the RG-6 than there is around the RG-59. The RG-6 can transmit the most signals, and thus, the most channels.
>
> The RG-6 is best for running cables underground and is usually used by the cable companies. For consumer use, the most common cable, and the one that hooks up to most components, is the RG-59.

Figure 1.2. A UHF/VHF/FM matching transformer.

☛ Push-on matching transformer. This is used for transforming a double-tipped flat wire into a round coaxial cable finish. This unit can be pushed on the input of the VCR (see Figure 1.3).

Figure 1.3. *A push-on matching transformer.*

- Signal splitter (see Figure 1.4). This is used for transforming a round coaxial cable into separate UHF and VHF bands, the VHF with a round coaxial-cable finish and the UHF with two screw-type finishes.

Figure 1.4. *A signal splitter.*

☛ Signal separator/cobimer (see Figure 1.4) used in antenna or rabbit ear connection. This gizmo has two functions. When turned one way it transforms round coaxial cables into separate UHF and VHF bands. The VHF has a round coaxial cable finish and the UHF has two screw type finishes. When turned the other way it transforms the separate UHF and VHF Bands into one coxial cable finish.

Figure 1.5   *A signal Separator/Combiner.*

If you find that you need accessories other than the ones listed here, look in the appendix at the end of this book. There you'll find a listing of the most common accessories. If you don't find it there, see your local electronics store manager.

How to Bag a VCR that Suits You to a "T"

How often have you bought more than you need of something? Probably about as often as you've purchased less than you need, if you're like most of us. The stakes are greater with media equipment, however, than with burger buns or grass seed. You'll be shelling out *the big bucks*. This may mean blunders on a large scale if you don't do your research first.

Read up first. Check the audio-visual magazines and *Consumer Reports*. Even though you may not understand all the lingo, you will have gone wading in the same waters in which you'll later learn to swim, if reading this book does its magic.

Then venture forth to the electronics shops. Plan on a foray to several, and expect to really quiz the socks off a few people. A word of warning about VCR salesmen. In my experience, most department-store salespeople know very little; the major electronics stores have knowledgeable clerks, but they'll be all over you like a bad suit because they're on commission. Big discount warehouses have the best deals, but you'll be adrift there without anyone to help you.

The best course is to go to several places for your information, find out which features most suit your video needs, *then shop prices*.

The basic two-head monophonic (not stereo) VCR is all Joe Blow needs for basic, run-of-the-mill recording and playback. All VCRs now come with remote control, as well as a technical refinement called "HQ" (for a high-quality picture with less noise), a camcorder jack, and on-screen programming. If you want something dressier, here are a few of the options you may want to include (or, in the final analysis, you may decide they're not worth the extra money).

☞ *Four heads are better than two.* But how much better? $100 worth, plus. They offer cleaner freeze-frames in extended play mode (EP), and may produce a slightly better picture during playback.

☞ *"Hi-fi stereo"—high fidelity stereo sound.* Most rented movies come in stereo; without a stereo VCR, you won't be able to hear it. On the other hand, maybe that effect isn't worth the extra 100-plus dollars to you.

☞ *Index-search.* This feature finds mid-tape passages quickly; along with the following feature, index-search is becoming standard.

- *VCRPlus*. This feature makes auto-programming easy as pie.

- *Tamper-proof tape door*. This is a nice feature for households full of busy-fingered children.

- *One-touch recording (OTR)*. In addition to the added convenience, a tape-time-remaining indicator eliminates the frustration of running out of tape five minutes before the end of the program.

- *Edit switch*. This feature boosts the signal when dubbing, to improve the quality of second-generation tapes.

- *Synchro-edit jack*. This allows you to connect to a camcorder or a second VCR.

- *Flying erase head*. This provides better, cleaner edits.

- *Jog-shuttle control*. This is an enhanced-playback control that is particularly handy for video editing. It lets you dial in the exact playback speed and direction.

- *Bar code programming*. You wave a wand over a preprinted swatch of bar code, and your VCR's programmed.

☞ *Super VHS (S-VHS).* This feature produces a sharper picture, and holds up better for multiple tape-to-tape copies (if you're that kind of enthusiast). Those who have a *source* of S-VHS pictures (such as the S-VHS camcorder) get the most out of this feature, for which you can expect to pay an additional $200-plus. The VCR must also be connected to a high-resolution TV set, preferably a model equipped with an S-video jack.

☞ *Digital effects.* VCRs equipped with digital-effects circuitry produce a sharp, clear image when you push the PAUSE button.

☞ *Newer formats (8mm and Hi8).* These formats are designed to accommodate a new breed of small camcorders, and they are not VHS-friendly.

Hope this briefing has helped you sort out some of the confusion surrounding VCR purchases. Happy hunting!

Lesson 2

Hooking Up a Cable-Ready VCR and Cable-Ready Television for Cable Reception

If you're an average city dweller, it's likely you have cable. Paying the monthly charge confirms this.

Before you hook up your VCR to your TV with cable, you must first determine whether both the VCR and TV are *cable-ready* and whether you need a cable box. If you already know (or if you find out while reading this chapter) that you do not have either a cable-ready TV or a cable-ready VCR, you need to skip to the next lesson on cable boxes.

Is Your TV Cable-Ready?

If your television is old and has two little screws on the back for attaching the VHF, it is not cable-ready; go on to the next lesson. But let's say you don't have a cable box and you want to see whether your newer set is cable-ready. If you know, or can find out in the manual, that your TV has a "TV/CATV" option, it is cable-ready.

First make sure your TV is in CATV mode. If your channels stop at 13, you are not in CATV mode. You are set up for an antenna; this is called *TV mode*. Ask your cable representative to see if you are receiving all the channels. If this isn't possible, take the plunge into your manual where the CATV mode is explained either under "Tuning" or "CATV." It will tell you how to change from the TV to CATV mode. Sometimes the television itself has a CATV/TV button. Other times it must be programmed to change modes. Again, if your TV has no CATV mode, you do not have a cable-ready TV.

Okay, you have no cable box and you're in CATV mode. Now turn on the set. The channels will automatically appear on-screen with the touch of a channel button. You'll see them fly by.

Your TV is cable-ready if you can see every channel provided to you by your cable company, either for their flat fee or special pay channels like HBO and Showtime. Confirm this by checking your TV listings or a list of channels from the cable company.

Is Your VCR Cable-Ready?

This process is much the same with the VCR. If the VCR is cable-ready, it will have both a TV and CATV mode. Look in the manual.

Either the TV/CATV button is on the actual box, or it can often be found in the auto-tuning menu. The information can appear on your television screen or directly in the VCR readout window.

Basic Cable Hookup to a Cable-Ready VCR and Cable-Ready TV

The following steps outline, step by step, the hookup process to allow you to use all (non-pay) cable channels for recording and watching at the same time, as long as both the VCR and TV sets can give you all the cable (CATV) channels in your area.

You'll need the following accessories:

- ☞ 1 coaxial cable

- ☞ TV

- ☞ VCR

Follow these steps:

1. Insert the cable that runs from the wall into the cable input found on the back of the VCR (see Figure 2.1). The cable input on the back of the VCR is a female coaxial input (with a needle hole in the middle) clearly labeled "IN."

2. Attach the extra coaxial cable to the VCR's "OUT" output. Attach the other end of the cable to the cable input on the back of the TV (usually labeled "cable/antenna" or "VHF/UHF") (see Figure 2.1).

3. Set the 3–4 selector found on the back of the VCR to "3." This determines which channel the VCR will support.

4. Make sure both the VCR and the TV are in CATV mode.

5. Set the VCR's TV/VCR control VCR so you will see the picture from VCR.

6. Congratulations! You have just hooked up your VCR and TV with cable. To test your hookup, turn both the TV and the VCR on and change the TV to channel 3. Use the channel selector on the VCR to change channels. The TV's picture should change. The apparatus that's the closest to the cable coming out of the wall, in this case the VCR, has control of the channel selection.

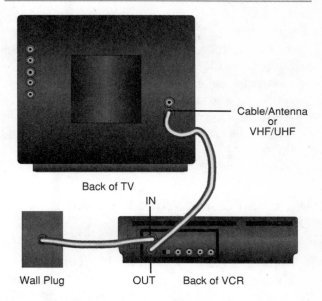

Cable/Antenna
or
VHF/UHF

Back of TV

IN

Wall Plug   OUT   Back of VCR

Figure 2.1 *Basic VCR and TV hookup.*

Tip

Why Channel 3? If you have cable, use channel 3. Almost all cable companies use 3 as the setting for their cable boxes and equipment. If you have it on 4, you will be one channel off on all channels. Unless specifically instructed in your manual or by your cable company, use 3.

Tip

Where Is It? Your VCR and TV may not have the inputs, outputs, and switches in the same places as depicted in these steps. All VCRs and TVs are a little different, so study yours very carefully. All of the inputs, outputs, and switches should be clearly identified.

Watching Oprah While Recording Donahue

Everything's in place. You've managed to mate the VCR, TV, and cable reception (see Figure 2.2). Now you are ready to record, and not only record, but watch another show at the same time.

Here's how:

1. Turn on the TV and the VCR.

2. Change the channel on the VCR to the channel you want to record.

3. Put the TV on channel 3.

4. Put a new or rewound tape into the VCR and put the VCR in VCR mode by pressing the VCR button (sometimes labeled TV/VCR).

5. Press the Record button on the front of the VCR; a "REC" message should appear somewhere on the display of the VCR.

Tip

Two for One Note that on some VCRs, you may have to press the Record and Play buttons at the same time to begin recording. Consult your VCR manual.

6. At this point, you'll be recording what you're watching on the TV. To record one channel and watch another, press the TV/VCR button so what you'll be seeing is coming from the TV.

7. Change the channel on the TV set to the channel you want to watch while the VCR continues to record the other channel to the end of the tape. The VCR will rewind the tape automatically.

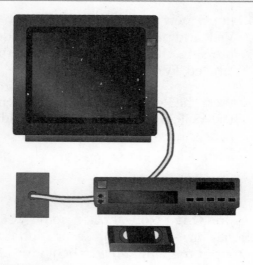

Figure 2.2 *Steps for recording.*

Old George

I got a call one day from a man who had been living in a senior citizens' apartment complex for two years. It seems that George wasn't satisfied with his cable TV reception. The cable company told him he was in a bad reception area. He asked me to come over and see if his hookup was correct.

I couldn't believe he had been trying to watch such bad reception (it looked like a snowstorm). He assured me the whole building was on cable. The hookup seemed okay, so I asked if his neighbors got good reception. He hesitated and said, "I don't know my neighbors . . . I keep pretty much to myself." Never the shy one, I suggested we knock on a few doors and see what kind of TV picture the people around him were getting.

We started out, George hanging back a bit, and discovered that everyone had the same problem. My suspicions were confirmed. The cable company had not provided a strong enough cable signal to the building. I called the public relations department of the cable company from George's phone (while he was out in the hall talking to his "new" friends). The cable company came out the next day with eight trucks and boosted the signal for the whole apartment complex (200 units), improving not only George's picture, but also everyone's picture.

Old George became a local hero. The last I heard from him, I got a postcard from Indiana. It seems the whole apartment complex had chipped in and paid for a trip for him to visit his sister he hadn't seen in 23 years!

Lesson 3

VCR Hookups with Cable Boxes: What a Great Place to Put a Potted Plant!

Tip

Attention! You do not need to read this chapter if you have a cable-ready VCR.

If you do not have a cable-ready TV and/or VCR, there is currently no way around it—You absolutely need a cable box in order to use the TV and VCR to their full potential.

Remember the basic premise of owning a VCR: The ability to record one channel while watching another. You can throw this premise, and your VCR with it, out the window if you introduce a cable box and install it in almost any way other than the one recommended here.

Other aspects of your viewing capability can also be undermined by an improper hookup, including the use of your TV set's remote control. Consider the price of the remote, anywhere from $50 to $75, squandered.

Beware of hookups suggested by cable companies, electronic stores, and neighbors. There are ways to maintain all your video functions with a cable box.

A Little Cable Box History

A cable box isn't just another electronic box of buttons designed to confound you. It was devised by cable companies to expand viewing options for cable subscribers with pre-cable televisions. Cable reception has swept the nation a lot faster than the need for new televisions. Older, pre-cable TV sets receive only twelve channels, 2-13, just a portion of the number offered through cable.

Cable boxes are separate tuners, making all cable channels accessible to a pre-cable TV set if that TV set is tuned to channel 3. It is easy to understand the cable companies' zeal in the original development of a cable box. Without it, only part of their product was available to most people.

The setup was simple:

1. Cable out of wall.

2. Cable into cable box.

3. Cable out of cable box and into TV set (tuned to channel 3).

However, this system does not allow you to use the remote control as intended for your TV set, since it's stuck on channel 3. You are obliged to:

- ☞ Get up to change the channels on your new cable box (unless you are paying extra for a cable box with a remote plus pay channels).

- ☞ Use your remote for volume only.

- ☞ Get up to make any other adjustments which had been on your TV remote control.

- ☞ Purchase a cable box with a remote control that offers sound and channel-changing capabilities.

So, that's $50–$75 worth of control buried in a junk drawer.

After receiving endless complaints and nasty letters from people who didn't want to get up off their butts to change channels, the cable companies offered a new cable box with its own remote control. Of course, the companies could not resist charging a monthly fee for this remote, and only a handful of companies made a remote control which could both change channels and adjust volume.

As a result, customers were left with two choices: they could pay the cable company to rent a cable box which unscrambled pay channels (and included a remote control which sometimes provided volume control), or they could receive at no charge a cable box which received the cable channels without a remote control, and continue to wear out the carpet between the set and the sofa.

More Cable Box Problems

Another enormous hurdle for the cable company was VCR technology. The VCR presents a problem not only because of the difficulty in determining audience ratings but also because of the proliferation of home-recorded video cassettes of major motion pictures. VCR technology is a scourge as far as the cable companies are concerned. So they've balked at developing a system which allows the customer to record a pay channel while watching another channel, and use their remotes.

Cable cooperation or not, nobody has been able to stop the relentless progress of the VCR, which now rivals, in sales, the TV set.

But customers still whine, "Here I am paying umpteen dollars a month. It's nice to have all the extra channels, but now I've bought a video cassette recorder, and I can't hook it up so that I can record a pay channel and still watch a regular channel at the same time. Also, I still have to keep my TV set on channel 3 because if I change TV channels, I don't get anything. When I see my expensive TV remote control in my junk drawer, it bugs me." But stay with me—yes, you *can* move your TV set off channel 3.

Friends, neighbors, and cable company employees are likely to suggest all manner of hookups which may or may not solve these deficiencies. Here are a few alternatives.

Cable Box Hookup for Those Who Don't Care About Remote Control or Watching One Channel While Recording Another

If your TV and VCR are not cable-ready, both you and the company that made it deserve congratulations for longevity. Unfortunately, your TV and VCR are both outdated—though not hopelessly, thanks to those basic accessories you learned about in Lesson 1.

You'll need the following accessories:

- ☛ 2 coaxial cables

- ☛ 1 matching transformer

- 1 cable box

- TV

- VCR

Follow these steps (see Figure 3.1):

1. Attach the cable box to the VCR antenna/cable IN with a coaxial cable, being careful to screw (or push) the cable terminal in hand-tight. Put the VCR on channel 3. The cable box, because it is the closest unit to the wall, will send cable channels through the VCR.

2. Attach a coaxial cable terminal to the back of the VCR at "OUT."

3. There are four small terminal screws on the back of your relic television: two that say "VHF" (very high frequency) and two that say "UHF" (ultra high frequency). (There is more information about VHF and UHF in Lesson 4.) One end of the matching transformer is a "female" terminal (if you can't see why it's called "female," you need to read an entirely different kind of book) to which you connect the outgoing cable from the VCR. The other end of the matching transformer has two wires with

metal "horseshoes" which attach to the VHF terminals on the television set. Loosen the two screws labeled VHF, place the "horseshoes" under the two screws and retighten the screws. Don't concern yourself with the UHF terminals because cable uses only VHF.

4. Turn the TV and VCR on and put the VCR on channel 3, too.

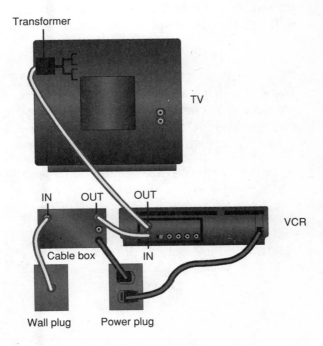

Figure 3.1 *A prehistoric cable box hookup.*

Cable Box Hookup Instructions for Those Who Do Want to Record One Show While Watching Another

It's easy to record the same channel you are watching, whether you're using a cable box or not. But let's find a way to record any channel, including pay, from the cable box, while watching any other channel directly from the TV set, and (ta-da!) using your TV remote control. To accomplish this miracle, you need to use either a device known as an A/B switch with a splitter or a control box.

The *A/B switch* is a 2-way switch that allows you to choose between two incoming signals (or by reversing it, to direct a single signal one of two ways).

A *splitter* is a device that allows you to send one signal two ways at the same time.

A *control box* is simply three or more A/B switches contained in one unit, allowing you to route a variety of signals.

You'll need the following accessories:

- ☛ 5 coaxial cables

- ☛ A-B switch

- ☛ splitter

- ☛ matching transformer

- ☛ cable box

- ☛ VCR

- ☛ TV

The hookup goes like this (see Figure 3.2):

1. Attach the cable from the wall into the two-way splitter.

2. Connect a coaxial cable from one output of the splitter into the "A" jack of A/B switch.

3. Attach a matching transformer to the back of the television. The end with the two little horseshoe wires is attached to

the two screws labeled "VHF" on the back of the television. Screw them down tightly. The matching transformer leaves you with a terminal compatible with your coaxial cables.

4. Connect another coaxial cable from the output of the A/B switch into the TV set's matching transformer.

5. Connect a coaxial cable from the other splitter output to the "IN" jack of the cable box.

6. Connect a cable from the cable box "OUT" jack to the "IN" jack on the VCR.

7. Connect the cable from the "OUT" jack of the VCR to the "B" jack of the A/B switch.

8. To confirm your installation, do the following. Turn on both the TV and VCR. With the A/B switch on A, you should be able to watch channels 2–13 on the TV set itself using the erstwhile useless TV remote with all its advantages. The couch potato is born! With

the A/B switch on B you can watch all
channels from the cable box including
pay and scrambled. Amazingly enough,
you will be able to record all channels
from the cable box.

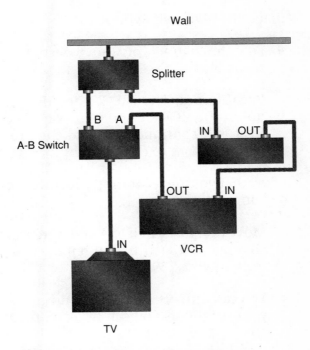

Figure 3.2 *A better switch box hookup.*

To Record for This Configuration

1. Turn on both the VCR and TV.

2. Put the VCR on channel 3. The VCR must also be in VCR mode.

3. Put the A/B switch on B.

4. Find the channel you want to record on the cable box.

5. Push Record. The "REC" should light up on the VCR's readout display. The VCR will continue to record the program through to completion.

Now that you are recording, you have the following options:

☛ Move the A/B switch to A and watch all channels 2–13 (with your remote control) on your TV set.

☛ You can turn off your TV set and go tell your neighbors you can hook up their sets for a small fee.

Using a Control (Switch) Box

The *control box* (also known as a *selector* or *switcher box*) is a prince among VCR accessories. It has proven to be the ultimate answer in providing the full range of uses to the

VCR, including the ability to watch and also record from the cable box. These are finally available at electronics supply stores, as well as from home improvement centers and some department stores.

After properly installing a control box, you'll be able to watch the TV set only and lord over your TV remote control for those channels. Plus you'll maintain the ability to watch any channel from the cable box.

You'll need the following accessories:

- ☛ 5 coaxial cables

- ☛ matching transformer

- ☛ cable box

- ☛ VCR

- ☛ TV set

- ☛ control box

- ☛ phono plugs

The hookup goes like this (see Figure 3.3):

1. Connect the cable from the wall into the cable/ant "IN" jack on the control box.

2. Attach a matching transformer to the back of the television. The end with the two little horseshoe wires is attached to the two screws labeled "VHF" on the back of the television. Screw them down tightly. The matching transformer leaves you with a terminal compatible with your coaxial cables.

3. Connect a cable from the control box jack labeled "INTO TV" to the "TV IN" jack on the TV's matching transformer.

4. Connect a cable from the control box jack labeled "TO VCR IN" to the "VCR IN" jack on the VCR.

5. Connect a cable from the control box jack labeled "TO VCR OUT" to the "VCR OUT" jack on the VCR.

6. Connect a cable from the control box jack labeled "AUX IN" to the cable box's "IN" jack.

7. Connect a cable from the control box jack labeled "AUX OUT" to the cable box "OUT" jack.

8. There is a phono plug input on the control box that says "GAME." This is connected to your video game "OUT." This makes it easy to plug in and tune out to the game.

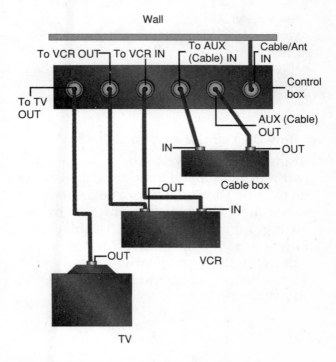

Figure 3.3   A control box hookup.

Combinations   If you have a cable-ready VCR but a pre-cable television, the installation is the same as above.

If you have a cable-ready television but a pre-cable VCR, the installation is the same except you do not need the matching transformer element in Step 2. Simply attach the cable directly from the control box to the television.

So, How Do You Use a Control Box?

Inside this control box are three A/B switches (without their metal casings) which are set up to move the signal from one component to another. This makes it possible, by following Table 3.1 exactly, to achieve the functions as listed. For example, to watch a video cassette, turn all switches up, set the TV to channel three, and leave the VCR on any channel.

Table 3.1. Control Box Settings

Functions	Switch Settings	Channel Settings TV	VCR
Watch TV set	6 up	Any	Off
Watch cable box (Pay TV)	2 and 4 down	3	Off
Play video games	All down	3	Off
Watch video cassette	All up	3	Any
Record a VCR channel	All up	3	Any
Record a VCR channel and watch cable box	2 and 4 down	3	Any
Record with cable box	3 down	3	3
Record with cable box and watch TV set	1, 3, and 5 down	Any	3

Lesson 4

Hooking Up the VCR to an Antenna

Antenna or Rabbit Ears: Why Do You Need Them?

Many roofs flaunt those wire contraptions called antennas. Rabbit ears (see Figure 4.1), the two telescoping wands that stick out of a single housing, are an indoor occurrence, most commonly featured on top of televisions. Both serve the same purpose: They intercept television signals in the form of waves. These signals move through the air invisibly as Ultra High Frequency (UHF) and Very High Frequency (VHF) waves. However, antennas do not receive as many channel signals as cable.

Properly installed, antennas and rabbit ears improve television reception. Antennas are measurably more efficient than the smaller rabbit ears because they are outside where the signals are. However some dwellings (like apartment buildings) don't have them, so people rely on rabbit ears. Moreover, in communities in which cable is available, cable companies air network television over their cables, thus eliminating the need for antennas or rabbit ears for cable subscribers.

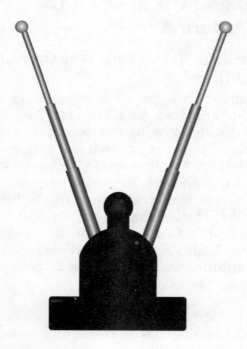

Figure 4.1 *Rabbit ears.*

UHF and VHF Television stations transmit electromagnetic waves through the air to your antenna or through the coaxial transmission line (cable) to your television.

Each station transmits on a different wave frequency. The frequency number is determined by the number of times the wave moves from one peak to the next in a single second; the higher the number of times, the higher the frequency. Ultra high frequency (UHF) is at the highest end; very high frequency (VHF) is in the middle.

Radio waves transmit on low frequencies. Television waves are transmitted through the air on the VHF band and the UHF band. When you select a channel on your television set, you are telling it which band to choose, UHF or VHF, and which channel within that band. Television is transmitted through cable only on VHF, not UHF. Cable television changes the location of these channels.

Tip

TV Reception from Beyond the Grave Just
when it looked like antennas were going the
way of the dinosaurs, a new development
has, at least temporarily, exhumed them.
Congress recently decided that local television stations can charge cable companies to
carry their transmissions. Since some cable
companies will balk at paying, antennas
may again be needed in households that
also subscribe to cable.

An Outdoor Antenna Properly Installed

One way to enhance the performance of
your antenna is to attach an electronic antenna rotor (see Figure 4.2). This will automatically rotate the antenna toward the
desired signal when you turn the dial to the
chosen channel.

Less costly is an arrangement where two
antennas are mounted facing transmission
from two different areas. In some cases, this
can work out very well. Ask an antenna
installer and your neighbors if the transmitters in your area are in different locations.
For instance, suppose channels 5, 6, 8, 10,
and 32 broadcast from the west, and 2, 7, 11,
and 54 from the east. Set up an antenna in
each direction, and by switching from one

antenna to another using an A/B switch, you could, achieve the following:

☛ Position 1—You would get good reception from 5, 6, 8, 10, and 32. At this point, the remaining channels in your area would be fair to poor.

☛ Position 2—You would get good reception on channels 2, 7, 11, and 54.

Figure 4.2 *An electronic antenna rotor.*

Let It Snow   Whether you use an antenna
rotor or switch antennas, you will have
problems recording one channel while viewing another at the same time if the signals
for both are not received from the same
direction.

Indoor Antennas or Rabbit Ears Properly Installed

Although the signal is not anywhere near as
clear as with an outdoor antenna, there have
been many improvements with respect to
reception from indoor antennas. The indoor antenna you purchase should be well
designed and equipped with a rotator dial.
Once you find, by experimentation, the best
position, you'll never again have to "wiggle
the ears." Switch to area locations numbered on the dial and receive somewhat the
same results as you would with an outdoor
antenna or antenna rotor.

To increase the strength of your incoming
signals, purchase an antenna amplifier at
your electronics store. The indoor antenna
or rabbit ears are attached to the amplifier

and the amplifier is then attached to the VCR in the same fashion as the antenna or rabbit ears.

Tip

Boost It! If added strength is needed on your outside antenna, use an antenna amplifier on the interior connection for that, too.

Making the Antenna or Rabbit Ears Compatible with Your Equipment

For the antenna or rabbit ears to work, both the VHF and UHF must be attached first to the VCR and the VCR must then be attached to the television.

The most frequent challenge in making these connections work is that the holes on the back of the VCR and the television are incompatible with each other, and with the wire or cable system from the antenna or VCR. For example, you might have two little wires on one end and a round orifice with a needle hole on the other. Or, you might find round cable with a tip like a hypodermic on one end and two little screws on the other.

Four Equipment Possibilities—
Four Solutions

Four possible configurations follow, with instructions for connecting antenna and rabbit ears to each:

The Ins and Outs Think of UHF and VHF coming out of the air and into your machinery. It is imperative that you bring it into the machinery at the places marked "UHF IN" and "VHF IN." When making the connections to move UHF and VHF out of one machine (into another), bring it out at the places marked "UHF OUT" and "VHF OUT."

☞ In Figure 4.3, the VHF and UHF signals leave the antenna on two separate flat wires. The VHF output is connected to a push-on matching transformer, and the signal enters the VCR at the RF input. The UHF signal enters the VCR at a double screw-type UHF input. The VHF signal is output from the VCR's RF output via a coaxial cable to the television's RF VHF input. The UHF signal is output from the VCR with a flat wire to the television's UHF input, a double screw-type.

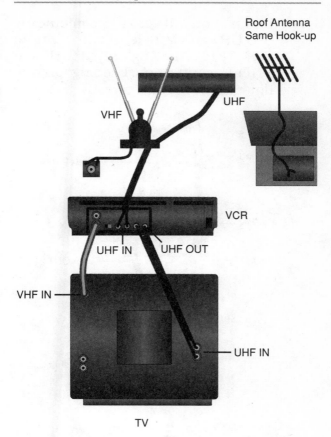

Figure 4.3 Antenna hookup with VCR and TV set.

☛ In case you have a new TV set that has but one RF input which combines UHF and VHF signals (no screw-type UHF

inputs), you will need to recombine the
two UHF and VHF leads coming from
the VCR into the single input (UHF and
VHF) TV connection. Use a signal combiner as shown in Figure 4.4.

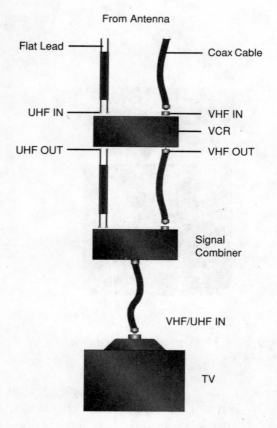

Figure 4.4 *Using a signal combiner.*

☞ Figure 4.5 shows the same antenna-to-VCR hookup as in Figure 4.4, but in this case, the VCR outputs are connected to a combiner, and carried by a single coaxial cable to the television's combined UHF-VHF input.

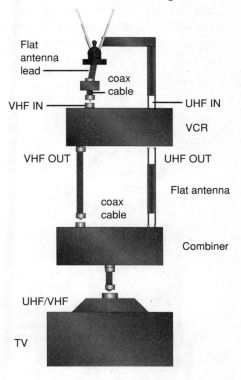

Figure 4.5   Using a combiner (a variation).

☞ In Figure 4.6, the antenna outputs are connected to a combiner and enter the VCR via a single coaxial cable. The signal leaves the VCR from the coaxial VHF output, and is connected to a decombiner. From the decombiner, the UHF signal enters the television at a double screw-type input and the VHF signal is carried via coaxial cable.

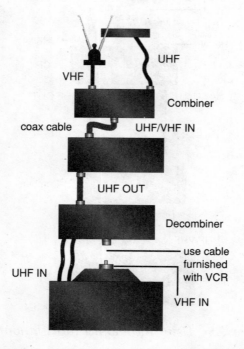

Figure 4.6 *Using a combiner and decombiner.*

Lesson 5

Hooking Up the VCR to a Satellite System

Can You Take What They Dish Out? To Beam or Not to Beam

If you have two backyards, deep pockets full of money, and a fanatical commitment to multiple TV viewing options, you may be a candidate for satellite reception.

Satellite Pros:

☛ If you live way out in the country, beyond the pale of antenna reception or cable access, a satellite may be your only way of being at one with the airwaves. Nothing—not tunnels, bridges, trees, skyscrapers, or mountains—interferes with your reception because the signal is beamed straight from space to your tube, via the satellite.

☛ You can receive many, many channels, paying no monthly fee. You'll have the airwaves of America, and sometimes beyond, at your fingertips, a real cocktail of offbeat possibilities—network show rehearsals, program feeds from NY to LA, and so on.

Satellite Cons:

☞ Satellite dishes are very, very expensive. Despite advertised claims, you can expect to pay $7000 plus for a dependable satellite dish and receiver. The receiver constitutes about half the cost. You need a receiver for each room in which you want a picture. You do the math.

☞ Never stunningly attractive, satellite dishes take up a tremendous amount of room. What looks jaunty on a lunar lander may not fit in with your flower beds at all. The requisite cement foundation will be there in perpetuity.

☞ Some zoning laws and neighborhood associations prohibit satellite dish installation.

☞ Satellite companies have a notoriously high mortality rate. Time and again people with so-called warranties call the company for service only to find they've pulled up stakes.

☛ The companion satellite-dish manual is roughly the weight and thickness of a major metropolitan telephone book. Operating a satellite system is extremely complicated; learning how to dish will be, in the beginning, a full-time job.

☛ If a satellite dish is inoperable, it is also non-disposable. Consider taking up topiary gardening.

Before You Shell Out for a Dish

If you live in the sticks and really need the one-eyed monster or just want to watch a kabillion channels, do the following before investing in a satellite:

☛ Check the zoning laws.

☛ Talk to people who have a satellite. Ask their opinion about the product, its performance, and the company from which they purchased it.

☛ Comparison shop, but don't exchange performance and company reliability for discount.

Wait for the Slim, Trim Option Currently, a flat plate dish is being used in Japan that is 24 inches square. This satellite dish, known as DBS (direct broadcast satellite) has not infiltrated the U.S. market, simply because the hugely powerful conglomerates that control cable companies and commercial networks recognize the threat of such easy-access TV. DBS systems use technology that could help bring high-definition TV to this country. They could also do away with video movie rentals. If and when these systems become available, the deep-dish satellite systems will go the way of the dodo.

The Antenna with Satellite Imperative

If you've got a satellite, you'll likely use an antenna too—you can't access local channels without one. Teaming an antenna with a satellite becomes absolutely imperative when you purchase a VCR. Without an antenna, you'll be able to receive only one channel at a time. You won't be able to watch one show and record another.

The Hookup Is the Easy Part

So, you've already battled your way through the mental anguish and expenditures, and you've installed a disfiguring monolith in your back forty. Figure 5.1 shows you the setup that will guarantee the maximum possible use of your VCR. And while these instructions look like a roadmap out of hell, they are not ultimately that complicated. Just start with the satellite end and work your way towards the TV. Remember: The TV must be on channel 3.

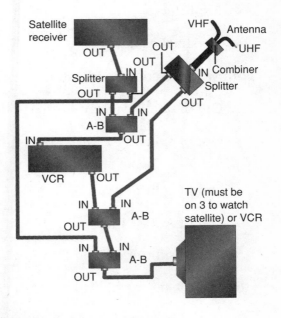

Figure 5.1. *A satellite hookup.*

You'll need the following:

- ☛ Satellite receiver and antenna

- ☛ VCR

- ☛ TV

- ☛ 3 A/B switches

- ☛ 2 splitters

- ☛ 9 coaxial cables

Follow these connection steps:

1. Out of satellite receiver into splitter #1.

2. Out of splitter #1 into A of A-B switch #1.

3. Out of splitter #1 into A of A-B #3.

4. Out of A-B #1 into VCR.

5. Out of splitter #2 into B of A-B #1.

6. Out of splitter #2 into B of A-B #2.

7. Out of VCR into A of A-B #2.

8. Out of A-B #2 into B of A-B #3.

9. Out of A-B #3 into TV.

Putting A/B Switches to Work for Your Viewing Needs

Table 5.1 shows you how to set up your A/B switches and television to get the most out of your equipment.

Table 5.1. Viewing Your Channels

To watch . . .	A/B switch	Setting
Antenna signal	2 and 3	B
Satellite signal	3	A
	TV	3
Antenna and record satellite signal	1	A
	2	B
	3	B
Satellite and record antenna	1	B
	3	A
	TV	3
What you are recording on the satellite	1	A
	2	A
	3	B
	TV	3
What you are recording on the antenna	1	B
	2	A
	3	B
	TV	3

Lesson 6

Tuning VCRs for Antenna and Cable Signals

Getting on the Same Wavelength

VCRs are a lot like TVs. They have their own tuners, either manual (pre-cable-ready) or automatic (cable-ready). The channels on your VCR must be matched and locked into assigned frequencies (whether VHF or UHF). Otherwise, your access to channels through the VCR will be lost in a miasma of overlapping signals.

Since the conception of VCRs, people have developed nasty calluses and torn out their hair trying to tune their machines to the airwaves. Subsequent improvements in VCRs have made tuning more simple, but many people still have first- and second-generation machines. This lesson will help you tune your VCR.

Different Types of VCRs and How to Tune Them

First-Generation VCRs

These antiques have 12 windows, which correspond to Channels 2–13. They were and are tunable by rotating little wheels, 2–6 for VL (very low frequency) and 7–13 for VHF (very high frequency). Once you find the channel with the wheel, that channel is tuned.

Second-Generation VCRs

Created in response to cable's plethora of channels, these VCRs are a real boondoggle. They usually have approximately 25 tunable channels—made for people with time on their hands, literally. To tune them, you first push the preset button. Next push the search button (either VHF or UHF). When you find the channel you are searching for, push the numbered buttons that correspond to the channels received. This will be confirmed in the display window on the front of the VCR. Then push the memory button to lock in each selection. Push the preset button off again, so your selections won't get lost.

These instructions are basic, but tuning methods vary from machine to machine.

Many people, daunted by complicated tuning methods, never find this information in their manuals and are still relegated to less than half the channels fed by their cable company. If you're still one of these after reading this, call your VCR's 800 number or talk to your electronics store representative.

Tip

Easy Tuning with Two TVs　If you receive cable and have two televisions, the easiest way to tune your VCR is to use a splitter. One of the televisions (TV *A*) must be cable-ready or you must have a cable box to accompany it. Divvy up the cable signal coming into the house with a splitter. Put one signal through to TV *A* on a coaxial cable. Put the other through to the VCR on a coaxial cable. Wire the VCR through to a second television (TV *B*) with another coaxial cable (see Figure 6.1). Put TV *A* on the desired channel, then slowly move through the channel search on the VCR. When the image on TV *B* corresponds to the image on TV *A*, the VCR is tuned.

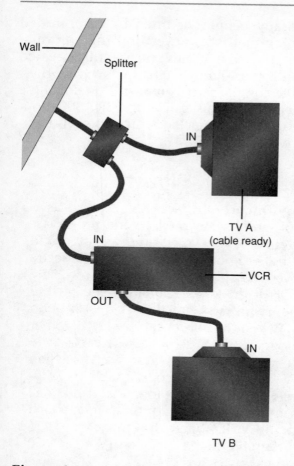

Figure 6.1. *Easy tuning of an older VCR, using two TV sets.*

Third-Generation VCRs

Hallelujah! VCR manufacturers must have realized they were losing customers to insane asylums. New cable-ready VCRs will automatically find and tune all cable channels if you know where to look for the TV/CATV (cable television) switch. Be sure to push it to get the full range of cable stations. If the TV/CATV button is not right on the box, it can often be found in the auto-tuning menu via the remote control. This information can appear on your television screen or directly in the VCR readout window.

If you're not in CATV mode, you're in TV mode. This allows you to receive antenna reception, and cable channels 1–13 only. Your third generation cable-ready VCR can tune all VHF and UHF channels in your area in each mode.

In Livid Color

There was a woman who called me for an appointment to hook up her new VCR. She seemed quite knowledgeable as we attached the cable to her VCR and, in turn, to her TV set.

continues

continued

When we finished, she said, "That's fine, but where is the color?" I explained to her that she would have to have a color TV set to receive color. She then became incensed at the salesman who had told her that the VCR would record and play back in color. (She neglected to mention to either of us that she still had a black-and-white TV.)

I then proved the point by attaching the VCR to a neighbor's color set.

Lesson 7

Using Two VCRs for Multiple Recording and Copying

The More, the Mightier: Multiple Births

If you want to see your pet videos multiplying like the proverbial bunnies, try the following. But first make sure that the outgoing coaxial cable from VCR I is attached to VCR II's "IN." Also, VCR II's "OUT" should be attached to the TV set (see Figure 7.1).

Follow these connection steps:

1. RF cable from wall into VCR #1.

2. RF cable out of VCR #1 into VCR #2.

3. RF cable out of VCR #2 into TV set.

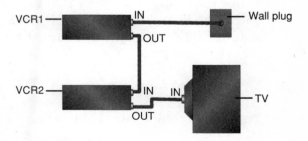

Figure 7.1. *Using two VCRs for multiple recording.*

To Record Two Different TV channels on VCR I and VCR II and Watch a Third:

1. Tune the TV set to Channel 3. Turn on VCR I and put it in VCR mode.

2. To confirm that VCR I is operating properly, change channels on VCR I and view them changing on the TV set.

3. Choose a channel to record on VCR I. You will see it on the TV screen.

4. Turn on the power on VCR II. Be sure VCR II is in VCR mode.

5. Switch VCR I to TV mode.

6. Choose a channel to record on VCR II.

7. Now, record both VCRs simultaneously and watch VCR II on the TV screen.

8. While recording, you can switch VCR II to TV mode and watch all basic channels on the TV screen at the same time the VCRs are recording.

To play back your tapes:

1. Put the TV set back on channel 3.

2. Rewind both VCR I and VCR II tapes.

3. Put the VCRs back in VCR mode and play back the tapes.

To Make a Copy from VCR I to VCR II

Commercial tapes may not copy properly, because they most often have a copy guard. If you wonder whether a commercial tape has a copy guard, the clerk in the video store won't be able to tell you. You may be able, however, to use your VERTICAL HOLD button to find out (you can find it on the back of your TV, or as part of the TUNER/BRIGHT-NESS/COLOR controls). By turning this control *slowly*, you can make black bars roll up or down your screen. Careful adjustment will hold the black bar in the center of your screen. If the bar is solid, there is no copy guard on the tape. If the bar has little numbers scribbled in it, there *is* a copy guard.

It is legal to copy tapes, but NOT to copy and sell them. (Homemade videos, on the other hand, can be subjected to many mul-tiplications.)

1. Insert a blank, rewound tape into VCR II.

2. Insert the tape to be copied into VCR I.

3. Both VCRs should be in VCR mode, not TV mode. Make sure that VCR mode is engaged on both machines.

4. VCR II must be on Channel 3.

5. Begin VCR II on "record" first.

6. A moment later, start playing VCR I.

7. Be sure to check the tape in VCR II for possible errors before recording the entire segment.

8. You can record in the opposite direction (VCR II to VCR I) by using the in and out patch cords as described in your manual. The only time this might be necessary is if VCR II has developed a recording problem, and will be used only for playing back. In that event, you may wish to play from VCR II and record on VCR I. (Of course, you could use the same system with RF connectors, and switch machines.)

To Make a Copy from VCR I to VCR II while Watching Another Program

Here is how to make copies and watch TV at the same time, using a splitter, an A/B switch, and two extra coaxial cables (see Figure 7.2).

1. Attach a splitter to the cable coming from the wall.

2. Connect a short cable from one part of the splitter to side B of the A/B switch.

3. Attach the remaining part of the splitter to the input on VCR I.

4. Attach a cable from VCR I's OUT to VCR II's IN.

5. Attach another cable from VCR II's OUT to the A part of the A/B switch.

6. Attach the center connection of the A/B switch to the TV set.

7. Proceed with 1 through 7 of the instructions for making copies from one VCR to another.

8. Turn the A/B switch to B to send the cable or antenna signal directly into the TV so you can watch the TV all you want.

If the A/B switch is on A, you'll be able to view what you're copying. Please note that without a cable-ready TV set, you would be limited to watching 12 channels. As mentioned previously, the cable company has provided for this by "loaning" you a cable box at no charge (or a small deposit).

> **Mega Copying!** You can make any number of copies using this system by adding more VCRs. However, if you use more than five at a time, you'll want to place a booster (amplifier) ahead of the second VCR.

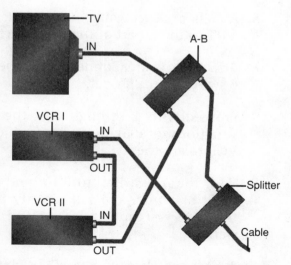

Figure 7.2. Make copies and watch TV using a splitter and an A/B switch.

If you have a control (switch) box as described at the end of Lesson 3, you will be able to make a copy from VCR I to VCR II, while watching the cable box (including pay TV). Figure 7.3 shows the arrangement.

Here are the steps:

1. Connect cable from wall to control box CABLE/ANTENNA IN.

2. Connect control box TV OUT to TV set IN.

3. Connect AUX/CABLE IN to cable box IN.

4. Connect AUX/CABLE OUT to cable box OUT.

5. Connect VCR IN to VCR I IN.

6. Connect VCR I OUT to VCR II IN.

7. Connect VCR II OUT to VCR OUT on control box.

On your control box, the switch setting would be all up; the TV set would be on channel 3. When you have started your recording or copying on VCRs I and II, you can push down 2 and 4 on the control box and watch TV through your cable box. When you play back a tape, put set the switches on the control box to all up.

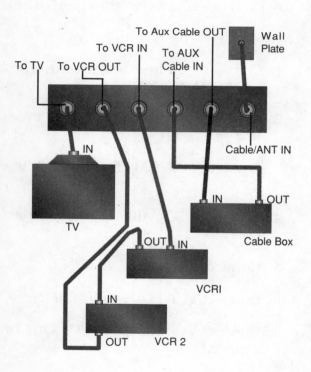

Figure 7.3 *Copy from VCR I to VCR II and watch a cable box (including pay TV).*

Lesson 8

Recording with the VCR

In this lesson, you'll find out about the VCR's many recording options. First, you'll review manual recording—about as complicated as pushing the button on a copy machine. Later, you'll move on to automatic programming—a great way to get your machines to do all the work while you're away. But before going into the recording methods, let's take a little detour to discuss tape speeds.

Go, Speed Racer! Why Faster Is Better

Let's talk cars. In general, the slower you drive, the better your mileage—that is, the longer your gas will last. But the faster you go, the more fun you'll have—that is, the greater the quality of your driving experience (anyone for *Fahrvergnugen*?). The same is true for your VCR: the slower the tape moves, the more hours you can record. But the faster the tape speed, the better the quality of the recording.

So before you start trotting out conspiracy theories to explain the missing hour at the end of your tape of *JFK,* it's important that you understand tape speeds and how they affect recording.

Learn to use your VCR's throttle; it has three speeds:

SP Standard Play gives you the best picture and goes the fastest (definitely what you want to record most of your movies on).

LP Long Play gives you twice as much time on the VCR and it works at half the speed of the Standard play and the picture is not quite as good. (This should be used when you are recording for a long period of time and you are not too concerned with the picture).

SLP or **EP** Superlong Play (Sometimes referred to as Extended Play). This gives you six hours of VCR time but the picture is much poorer than the picture you can get with Standard Play).

You can choose a recording speed by pushing the button on the exterior of your VCR. It's recommended that you not drive your machine any slower than the SP (2 hour) mode for the best quality recording. The faster the tape revs, the better the recording (SP is best, LP is next best, EP or SLP is worst). There may be instances in which the loss in quality doesn't bother you—like you're going to be gone for six hours come hell or high water so you have no alternative but to use SLP.

If while recording at SP speed, you realize you won't have enough tape for the entire program, you can change to a slower speed by pushing the LP or EP/SPL buttons without disturbing the recording.

For example, on standard play (SP) most videocassette tapes last two hours. For a longer program (over two hours), you need to enact the LP or EP speed.

Tip

Another available VHS cassette tape, code number T160, allows four, six, and even eight hours of recording. The added length is possible because the actual tape is thinner. Since T160 tape was introduced, I have heard no complaints on it except for the price. The entire tape-handling structure of the VCR appears to be more stable than that of audio-cassette equipment. Be forewarned, however, that the drive mechanism on a VCR is often the first component to go. Get in the habit of using a separate rewinder.

Standard Programming: Keep That Michael Jackson Video to Watch Over and Over Again

Let's review standard recording procedure. This is what you do when you are nestled down in front of your electronic hearth and want to duplicate what's coming over the waves:

1. Make sure the TV is tuned to channel 3.

2. Insert the rewound tape into the VCR and set the counter reset button to zero.

3. Confirm that the VCR is in VCR mode. (There is a button on the VCR, and usually one on the VCR's remote, called VCR/TV). The VCR is not always in the VCR mode when turned on. If you are seeing channel three, your VCR is in TV mode. To fix that, push the button.

   Change the channels on the VCR or with the VCR remote control. If the channel changes, you're ready to go.

4. Push Record (or Play and Record if you have an older VCR).

Automatic Programming: Recording Oprah while Playing Tennis

This is like automatic pilot, and lets you be in two places at the same time. You'll love it.

"On-screen programming" means the VCR shows a menu on the TV screen. The menu walks you through the process of making programming dates for your VCR, choosing times and dates for programs you want to record, up to several days or weeks in advance.

On-screen programming merely indicates a significant advance in making programming easier. Even before it was developed, VCRs always had the capability of being programmed. If yours has a clock and a number of programmable channels, it can be set to do its job while you're away. You will need to consult the VCR's manual, and proceed with vast patience.

1. Make sure the TV is tuned to channel 3.

2. Insert the rewound tape into the VCR and set the counter reset button to zero.

3. Go to the kitchen and get a bottle of Gatorade to bring with you to the tennis match so that you don't dehydrate.

4. Go back to the living room and confirm that the VCR is in the VCR mode. Change the channels directly on the VCR or with the VCR remote control. If the channel changes you are all set.

5. Push the Program button (On some VCRs you may only find it on the remote control). Observe the readout on the VCR or TV screen.

6. Choose a program number 1–8.

7. Select the day, date, start time, end time, and channel number.

8. When you've finished programming one or more channels, push the Timer button or turn off the VCR. In either case, there will be a light that denotes the timer.

9. It's important to know that just because your VCR is programmed in advance, you are not deprived of its regular use. The VCR has been taken over by a computerlike device which controls the VCR for starting and stopping only as you have programmed it. Therefore, use it

anytime you like except during the time when you have a program scheduled to record. After automatic programming your VCR, don't forget to have a tape in the VCR and have the VCR off and/or the Timer button turned on.

For Brave Souls   Often you will see a blinking light which indicates the order of selection. When you have finished setting program 1 (and you're feeling confident), you may want to choose another program to record. You are able to record the same or another channel at different times. You can program the same show daily or once a week—even weeks in advance on some VCRs.

VCRPlus and Other Programming Aids for Non-Programmers   This on-screen programming is pretty tricky for many of us. Manufacturers move at a snail's pace toward friendly interfaces. One such move is VCRPlus. Widely sold separately for about $60, VCRPlus now also comes incorporated into many VCRs. It uses the special three- to seven-digit program code that appears in the newspaper TV listings.

continues

continued

The ever-clever Japanese have come up with a separate remote just for programming. You plunk each piece of basic information onto the display—date, start time, stop time, and channel, and then send the information to the VCR with the Transmit button. These remotes work with dials rather than buttons, probably because dials are considered old-fashioned and therefore more friendly. So you can now end up wrangling four different remotes, one each for your TV, VCR, cable box, and programming function.

Programming Pitfalls

Have you ever said, "But I wanted to record the game—not the home shopping channel!"? The following are problems that most people find in programming VCRs and tips for avoiding them. Most of these problems and solutions are not covered in the manual.

☞ Rewind the video cassette to the beginning (programming a cassette in the middle may make you think you haven't automatically recorded it all).

☞ When you have finished programming one or more channels, push the Timer button or turn off the VCR. In either case, there will be a light that denotes the timer.

☛ Avoid unpleasant surprises later by practicing short, five-and ten-minute programming runs so that you can observe the accuracy of your work.

☛ Most VCRs allow you to check your program(s) prior to or during the program run. This is spelled out in your manual. However, normally by pushing the Program button, you will see a readout for those programs you selected so you can double-check your work.

☛ Pushing the Record button puts the record function on automatic programmer and sends the operating signal back to the TV set so you can watch other programs while your VCR is recording. Or you can just turn off the TV set if you go to bed and the VCR will keep recording. When you come back to watch what you've recorded, don't forget to put the VCR/TV function back in VCR.

☛ Remember, you are not deprived of your VCR's regular use just because it has a date with the airwaves. The VCR has been taken over by a computer-like device which controls the VCR for starting and stopping only as you have programmed it. Therefore, use it anytime you like except during the time when you have a program scheduled to record. After automatic programming your VCR, don't forget to have a tape in the VCR and have the VCR off and/or the Timer button turned on.

☛ It is never necessary to have the TV set turned on while your VCR is taping, unless, of course you are watching TV (for some people, it's not necessary even then).

Express Recording

For those last-minute, split-second decisions to record, most VCRs have yet another recording button to push. Most companies call it the XPR (express recording) button. This feature allows you to begin the recording at once, on the spur of the moment.

The recording time is determined by the number of times you press the XPR button. Each time you press the button, the VCR increases the recording time by one-half hour. So, to record "Roseanne," press the button once. To record "60 Minutes," press the button twice. For "Colombo," four times. You can press the button up to eight times, for up to four hours of recording.

When you use this feature, don't use the automatic programming features. Just be sure the VCR is on Record (check the display) and that you have chosen the channel you want. To stop express recording, keep pushing the button until the read out on the VCR or TV screen says "0 0 0 0."

Lesson 9

The Care and Feeding of VCRs

Ask any VCR repairman. Almost any calamity can and does happen to VCRs. VCRs eat videotapes. Videotapes eat VCRs. Marbles, pizzas, bubble gum, hair, peas, audio cassette tapes—all manner of objects—find their way into the loading mechanism. It's a slot, and slots invite filling. People spill drinks and meals of every viscosity on top of VCRs. It's almost routine. VCRs get dropped, dipped, and even melted. Even if you're a tidy, careful person, owning expensive equipment provides its own minefield of potential disasters. Avoiding them is your imperative.

Prevention

Know your machine to the nth degree. This means thoroughly digesting the instruction manual and this book, if you can stomach it. If you know what your VCR can do, you'll better understand what it can't do. This way you won't be tempted to push and prod it into a state of collapse.

Children of any age are, of course, a VCR's primary (and most inventive) enemies. Little kids, toddlers especially, actually fall into the predator category. First the buttons beckon kids to push them. When they discover that pushing the buttons makes lights go on and off, toddlers go ape, putting aside anything Fisher Price in favor of Mom and Dad's media lifeline. It's only a matter of seconds before the cunning little trolls have their fingers through the door of the loading mechanism and are busily installing whatever will fit.

So, the first lesson in the care of a VCR is to keep it well out of reach of small children. As soon as your child is within the age of reason, teach him or her how to care for and operate the VCR. The best way to do this is by example. If you treat the machine like a Ferrari, your child will be more inclined to do likewise.

Keep the VCR as far off the floor as possible, and covered when not in use. This will solve the kid problem, and minimize the amount of lint and dust it takes in.

Keep the VCR and the rest of your electronic equipment in a closed cabinet when not using it. Again, less debris is absorbed.

Make sure your cables are not bent or pulled. The surplus allowance between machines and the wall should be loosely wound and stored where they won't be tripped over. Tripping over them will yank the cable, or worse, pull your machines onto the floor.

Keep Your Machine Squeaky Clean

The Exterior

Every few days take a dry cloth and wipe each section. Don't use an oily dusting spray like one for wooden furniture, since this will attract dust. Use a soft, sable painter's brush for hard-to-reach places like the ventilation slots.

If the machine is particularly gross, use a mild spray of a household cleaning product. Don't go hog-wild and spray the VCR itself since excess can drip inside and may damage the infinite complications within. Put the product on a sponge or cloth; then wipe the cabinet.

Electronics supply stores sell a basic degreasing solvent in a spray can, a mixture of Freon and alcohol. Freon, the coolant used in air conditioners, is a great grime-busting agent because it dries without residue. Use this spray to clean the more delicate areas of the VCR cabinet where interior elements may be exposed.

Never use cleaner with an acetone or petroleum base, since it might remove paint or damage the plastic.

The Interior

Just like audio cassette decks, VCRs use spinning magnetic heads to record and play tape. *Magnetic* is a key word here. When the tape moves through, its oxide coating attaches to the heads, together with any other dirt or contaminants within the area. Dirty heads make for dicey images—anything from an occasional blur to a blizzard. The heads need routine cleaning, every month or two.

You can do this yourself. Commercially-manufactured cleaning cassettes are not hard to find; they even have them at your local drugstore. Scotch brand video-head cassette cleaners are the only ones I recommend. They are a new and better system—in fact (as I've mentioned before), a breakthrough. This product *is* being licensed to other companies, but for now, I suggest you specify the Scotch product. It costs a little more, but the results are worth it.

If, for some reason, you can't locate the Scotch brand, be sure to buy the "wet" rather than "dry" variety of cassette cleaners. You just put a drop or two of the liquid cleaner that comes with it on the tape, and then pop the cassette into the machine and play it for the 20-seconds-or-so recommended time. Do not overdo this type of cleaning since it is possible to wear down a video head by using a cleaning cassette.

Submit your VCR to regular professional maintenance and cleaning. Once yearly is enough for most VCRs. But if yours is exposed to heavy doses of dust and grime, or if it is kept in a humid location, you'll need more frequent cleaning. Make haste to your electronics repairperson or service facility if:

☛ You (or someone you used to love) drops the machine. Even if there is no visible hemorrhaging, plugging in the machine and playing a tape might cause additional damage.

☛ Your VCR is exposed to fire, smoke, or heat above 150 degrees.

☛ You spill anything inside—liquids and solids inclusive. Even if the VCR seems okay, playing it may send it over the edge.

- The picture and sound aren't as clear as they used to be.

- The machine makes unusual sounds.

- The outside is very dirty. The inside will be dirty too.

Tip

Warning, Will Robinson! I know the following admonitions will not apply universally, but if the warning fits, heed it. Reading this book may build your confidence to such an extent that you may feel ready to clean your own machine. (I know this sounds like a departure from sanity to most of you). Before you get out your Phillips head and start untwisting the little screws that will unveil your machine's interior, know this first: Taking apart and working with the interior of your VCR voids your warranty. It is also complex and requires its own manual.

Everyone knows that turning the power off and unplugging the machine before taking the cover off is imperative. Even with the power off, electricity is still present at the terminals near the unit's power supply unless the VCR is unplugged. If your machine is an AC-operated home model, removing the cover exposes 110 or more volts of alternating current; this current can kill you.

You might want to keep a logbook indicating when and where your VCR is serviced and when you use the head-cleaning cassettes.

The Remote Control

If your VCR gets groady, your remote control gets groadier. It's regularly put through its paces by every sweaty palm in the house, hands that are one with chips, dips, popsicles, and chocolates. Clean the exterior of your remote control in the same way you clean the exterior of the VCR, only more often. Since remotes run on batteries, the battery contacts are apt to become dirty. Every once in a while, remove the batteries and clean the contacts with the tip of a pencil eraser. If you find battery acid on the interior, throw away the batteries and remove the acid with a damp cloth. This stuff isn't called *acid* for nothing.

Eliminate Extended Warranties

Murphy's Law seems particularly applicable to warranties; machines always break within a month of when they expire. Why not have your VCR cleaned and inspected during the final months of warranty coverage, for free?

Prudence, routine cleaning, and maintenance cost far less than extended warranties.

Building Your Video Tape Bank

Like everything else, tapes have their own life span. Here are a few tips for contributing to their longevity:

1. Store the tapes in a cool, dry place away from direct sunlight, in an upright position.

2. Keep them off the floor, away from dust, lint, and fibers.

3. Keep them several feet away from electronic sources such as televisions, telephones, and loudspeakers. The magnetic field surrounding electronic equipment can zap the contents of the tape.

4. Keep them away from small children. Teach your children how to care for them properly.

5. Never touch the tape surface.

6. Repair cracked plastic tape cartridges using a small amount of modeler's cement on a brush. Do not apply too much cement or it might drip onto the tape inside. If the cartridges is really creamed, get a professional to transfer the tape to another cartridge.

The Case of the Fuzzy Wuzzy VCR

The man on the phone explained to me that he just couldn't get his VCR going. Said it was new and had never been used. He added that he'd just been through a divorce—he and his ex-wife were just now dividing up the physical assets and the VCR was his.

I don't like to check out new equipment for fear of voiding the warranties, but all he was asking me to do was push a few buttons and look it over. When I arrived he led me to a closet where several fur coats were hanging. The VCR was on a top shelf and not in a box. I asked him if that's where he had always kept the VCR and he said "Yes." (I did a mental cringe.) He reached up with his six-foot-four frame and brought the VCR, along with lots of dust and fur, down and put it on a table.

continues

continued

"Tell me again, how old is this VCR?" I asked.

"Like I told you before, brand new—never been used," he answered.

"But when did you actually buy it?"

He then clarified the matter by explaining that the VCR had been a wedding gift two years ago, and they had never gotten around to using it. Just took it out of the box and put it in the closet. I told him he was in for a big surprise. As I spoke, I took the top off and there it was. Dracula's castle filled with dirt, dust, and fur.

Did you know that VCRs have a magnetic quality of greater strength than anything except a magnet itself?

Two years in a closet without a cover and no fur coats is bad enough. But with fur coats— bad news! I told him all was not lost, but to take the VCR to a reputable repair place for a complete cleaning.

We were laughing at this point, so I suggested he try to work out a financial settlement with his wife—oops, ex-wife—on the repair bill.

Lesson 10

Sending Signals to Other Rooms

Listen. Not every television in your house needs its own battery of company-installed cable hookups and VCRs. Everybody tells me they want to hear more about saving money. So, let's talk more about saving money. One way is to use only one VCR for all the TVs in your home or apartment. Yes, you can use your VCR to show movies on as many TVs in your home as you like. And while you're at it, you can send the cable signal to those same rooms, without extra charges.

You can save the monthly costs the cable company charges you for additional outlets. Let's say you're paying $6.00 per month for each of the two extra rooms. At $12.00 per month times 12 months, you'll save $144.00 a year. Not bad!

There will of course be an extra charge for the pay channels—but there's no need to pay that extra charge for each TV set.

Let's say that you have three rooms with TVs, or you may have one room with three

TVs. One VCR can service all these rooms and all these TVs.

Linking the Cable to Every TV in Your House without Paying the Cable Company for Each Hookup

He likes Showtime, she likes Lifetime. Now both of you can have his-and-hers wiring. Let's discuss how to bring your cable signal to all the rooms you want. You have two options. You can use one line or two. The hookup instructions and illustrations are following.

Tip

Cable Ready or Not! The following in-structions are for cable-ready TVs only. If you have a pre-cable TV, your best bet it to purchase a control box (described in Lesson 3), to operate the cable box and other functions.

A One-Line Hookup

You'll need the following accessories:

- ☛ Splitters—as many as you have televisions

- ☛ TVs

☛ VCR

☛ Coaxial cables—twice as many as you have TVs plus two more; in other words, if you have three TVs, you need eight cables (the length of the cable will depend on the distance between rooms)

Steps to hook up one cable line to all rooms (see Figure 10.1):

1. Attach 3-way splitter to cable from wall.

2. Attach one cable to splitter and go into A of A-B switch #1.

3. Attach middle of A-B switch to TV set.

4. Attach a cable to another part of 3-way splitter to IN on VCR.

5. Attach a cable from OUT on VCR to input of 2-way splitter.

6. From one part of 2-way splitter to B of A-B switch #1.

7. From next part of 2-way splitter to B of A-B switch #2.

8. Third part of original 3-way splitter goes to A of A-B switch #2.

9. Come out of A-B #2 and go to other room with cable.

10. Attach this cable to a 2-way splitter (hide it behind a door or whatever).

11. Go from one part of this 2-way splitter to TV #2.

12. Attach cable to second part of splitter and go to the room with TV #3. You can continue to split the cable to attach to another room and so on.

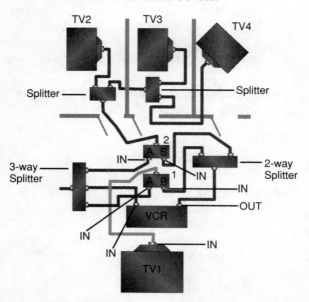

Figure 10.1. *Sending cable to other TVs using one line.*

More Power to You. If the picture gets snowy, install a booster on the cable where it first comes out of the original wall, before the splitter.

A Two-Line Hookup

For this hookup you will need:

- ☞ Control (switcher) box

- ☞ Cable box

- ☞ VCR

- ☞ TV

- ☞ Six splitters

- ☞ Two A-B switches

Follow these steps (see Figure 10.2):

1. From your control box "to TV in" go to TV in.

2. From your control box "to VCR out" go to one side of splitter #2.

3. From your control box "to VCR in" go to VCR in.

4. From your control box "to Aux cable in" go into cable box in.

5. From your control box "to Aux cable out" go into cable box out.

6. From your cable box "cable/aux in" go to one side of splitter #2.

7. From middle of splitter #1 go to out on VCR.

8. Cable from wall goes to middle of splitter #2.

Now we're off to the other rooms.

9. From other side of splitter #1, go into middle of splitter B in first room.

10. From other side of splitter #2, go into middle of splitter A in first room.

11. One side of splitter A goes into A of A-B switch.

12. One side of splitter B goes into B of A-B switch.

13. Middle of A-B switch goes into TV 2.

14. Run a line from open sife of splitter A to the next room and attach to middle of splitter A.

15. Run a line from open side of splitter B to the next room and attach to middle of splitter B.

16. One side of splitter A goes to A of A-B switch in this second room.

17. One side of splitter B goes to B of A-B switch in this second room.

18. Middle of A-B switch goes to TV in second room.

From the two extra rooms when A-B is on A you'll pick up cable, when A-B switch is on B you get whatever is on the VCR.

So, How Does It Work?

After hooking up the cable to all of the rooms, you're probably wondering how to watch TV and movies. This section will give some scenarios and solutions.

☛ You just brought home a new Demi Moore movie. Your daughter is in bedroom #1 and wants to see it. This is what you do:

Put all slide switches up on the control box. Put the movie into the VCR, put the TV on 3 and VCR on VCR mode. Run the movie up to titles and check on your main TV. Tell your daughter to put her set on Channel 3 and start playing. (Her A-B switch must be on B.)

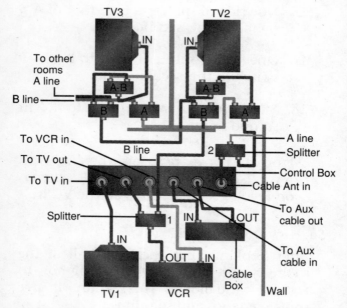

Figure 10.2   Sending cable to other TVs using two lines.

☞ Your mother is in bedroom #2 and wants to watch "Murder She Wrote." All she has to do is turn on the TV and have A-B switch on A.

☞ It's now 8 p.m. and everything is running smoothly, but you'd like to watch the Discovery Channel. Take the remote and click to that channel. Put 2 and 4 down on the control box and watch any channel coming from the cable box (regular or pay). At this point you can watch anything. Your daughter can watch her movie or move the A-B switch to A and watch anything except pay TV.

☞ If Grandma wants to see the Demi Moore movie, all she has to do is move the A-B switch to B and the TV to 3.

☞ There is a good movie coming on Showtime that Jamie wants to see. This is how you send a pay channel to her room:

Go to the channel box and put 3 down and the rest up.

Push Channel 2 on the VCR (in the VCR mode).

Push Channel 43 or ? on the cable box and Channel 3 on your TV set.

At this time you will see the Showtime move being billboarded and your daughter will be seeing the same thing, if she has her A-B switch on B and TV on Channel 3.

☛ Grandma is staying up for Letterman so set her A-B switch on A for cable. You want to see Letterman, too — so you push 1, 3 and 5 down on the control box.

Common Questions About Splitting to Other Rooms

If I'm sending movies to all the rooms from one VCR, why don't I use one of those transmitter devices?

Why pay $100 when you can get a better picture for next to nothing? Transmitter devices were brought on the market several years ago. They are like mini-transmitters— too small for a mountaintop, but just right for on top of personal electronics. The problem is that they are legally limited to transmit only 25 feet because they interfere with the neighbors' TVs. They get snowy after that (the transmitters, not the neighbors).

What are the legal problems of not paying the cable company for the other TVs attached to cable in your home?

None. The assessor's office is responsible for the annual appraisal of all cable TV franchises. To quote: "The line inside the home or apartment belongs to the property owner." However, this also means that the cable company is not responsible for work done by you or a video consultant.

If I have cable-ready TVs in the other rooms, can I watch all channels being sent from the main cable in the main room?

Yes.

I don't have a cable-ready TV. Can I watch all the channels?

Nope. You'll need a cable box. If you didn't receive a free (deposit-only) cable box from your cable company, call now and say, "I'd like my cable box. Where do I pick it up or could you deliver it?" If you want pay channels, there will be a monthly charge, but you should have a free cable box no matter what.

You can buy cable boxes for the other non-cable-ready TVs and then receive all the channels on those TVs as well.

If the cable company doesn't give me enough power for three TV sets, should I buy a booster?

First, call the cable company and ask them to bring out a strength meter. They are legally obligated to give the proper amount of power (0 to +5 db).

If you do add a booster, it should be in front of everything else. Cable out of wall, then the booster, then all your other equipment.

Using a Cable Box

Now you have a free cable box. Choose one of your other non-cable-ready (pre-cable) TVs and attach the main cable that has been split to this room to the input of the cable box, and then from the output to the TV set. With your TV on Channel 3, you'll have all the regular cable channels.

For the remaining non-cable-ready TV sets, you can either buy another cable box (from your local electronics store) or use the VCR channels in the same way as you view a movie; that is, put your TV set on 3 and choose the channels above 13 you need from the VCR tuner in the main room.

Squirreling Away the Cables Themselves

Now, you have hooked up all three TVs in all three rooms and you have black cables all over the floor. Here's how to hide them.

Tip

Hide the Cable. I'm not in favor of having the cable go outside the house and then back inside to the next room. What a mess. You'll spend a lot of time and money drilling holes in the house, creating new entrances for unsavory wildlife. It's much better and easier to secret away your cable web indoors.

Ideally, you have wall-to-wall carpeting. The carpet edge is pounded into a tack strip (the little gully between the floor and the wall) and the tack strip is not flush against the wall. This is where the cable goes (see Figure 10.3). It's as though floors were created for cable!

You need pliers, a spatula, wire strippers, a crimper, electrician's tape, a yardstick, a lot of coaxial cable, and some f-connectors (those little metal "male" ends for the cable). Bring the carpet up at the edge very slightly. Use the pliers just to test it, and you'll see it will come up where the tacks are. (This doesn't ruin the carpet.) Do a yard or two at a time. Lift the carpet, lay in some cable, and put carpet back down onto the tack strip. The tool of choice is a spatula. It will help push the carpet back down under the molding.

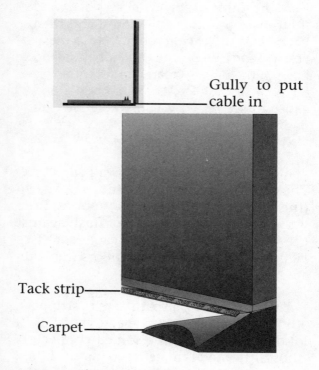

Gully to put cable in

Tack strip

Carpet

Figure 10.3. *Hiding the cable.*

Tip

Wooden Floor Dilemma! Don't worry if you have wooden floors. You could drill a small hole in the floor and run the cable through the basement or crawlspace. Attach the cable to the floor joists so it doesn't hang.

Plan ahead when you're measuring cable so that the splitters will be behind a door or somewhere out of sight. Any A-B switch used in this system should be located next to, or on, the TV set (double-stick tape works great for this).

Passing Through the Doorway

Don't panic!

Get out the yardstick. Wrap the end of the cable to the end of the yardstick. Use black electrician's tape for this because you don't want the cable to come off. When you bring up the carpet and before you get to the doorway itself, insert the yardstick with cable attached and push it through to the other side of the door. Pull up the carpet and pull it through. Undo the yardstick.

Using the wire stripper and crimpers, attach the f-connectors to the cable ends after the full length is laid and you are standing there next to your machines.

Of course, there's no electricity going through this cable. Some people are worried about this, but I assure you, there's no danger using coaxial cable in this way.

Over-Qualified

During one episode of hiding the cable under wall-to-wall carpeting, I suddenly found myself working with Pedro, a professional carpet installer. He was practically at my side and tacking down the carpet edge while I was a few feet behind him pulling it up and installing cable.

Understandably, Pedro took a dim view of this procedure. My actions had been OK'd by the home owner, but he had neglected to inform Pedro who had been scheduled to install new carpet on the same date.

The idea of one person tacking carpet edge followed by another person pulling it up did seem a bit unreasonable, but then I showed Pedro how a cable could be inserted in the groove behind the tack strip next to the wall. I then demonstrated how the carpet would be returned to its original position as previously tacked.

Pedro watched me closely, and suddenly he became very friendly.

"Jim," asked Pedro, "Do you mind if I ask your age?" .... "You do very good work, Jim, but I'm sorry, you're too old to be my apprentice. Let's just change places."

Lesson 11

Big-Screen Projection TV

Viewers who hanker to watch something bigger than a microwave may opt for projection TV, aka "big-screen TV." Hooked up to your VCR big-screen TV recreates the theater atmosphere.

Although big-screen TV is bigger, it's not any more cumbersome to install than a regular television. You actually hook up your big-screen the same way you would hook up your 19-inch set—of course, you'll probably be a lot happier about doing it.

If the results of your big-screen hookup are blurred in the extreme, you've done it wrong. Here are some general-info tips on big-screen TVs that'll help you make your picture as clear and sharp as if you were at the theater.

There are two basic kinds of projection TV:

Self-contained This type has a TV projector inside the cabinet and yes, it's all done with mirrors. The beam is bounced off two mirrors and then to the rear screen.

(If the set used only one mirror, you'd see the picture inside out.)

Two-piece units   This includes the projector and a separate screen. The newer ones can be focused so you are no longer obligated to have the screen at an exact distance from the projector.

Projection TVs use a wonderful little feature called *convergence*. This means that all of the color is filtered correctly so that it looks consistent on the screen. When the color is not "converged," half of Sylvester Stallone's face might be yellow and half might be green. All TVs have a convergence feature, but on projection TVs, you can adjust it yourself, preclude a repairman, and save plenty moola. Look in your manual to see where this feature is located among the many buttons on your projection TV. The button may say "test." When you push it, a fine-line cross will appear on the screen. If your set needs to be converged, there will be color ghosting, which means several different colors will appear, along the lines of the cross. Fiddle with the four buttons that are located next to the test button. Your objective is to make that fine-line cross pure white. Once you've done this, your picture will be much improved.

Good Eye-to-Screen Ratio

If you went to a large movie theater and sat in the front row, the picture wouldn't be clear. The same is true of big-screen TVs. Your picture will seem much better if you sit 15 to 20 feet away from a 50-inch set. In most stores selling big screens, you can't get far enough away to appreciate how good the picture can be.

Placement

It's really important not to place your big-screen projection TV facing a window—the light washes out the picture and you'll begin to question your investment. Figure out where you're going to to put your set before the thing is delivered, preferably in the daytime, so you can see how light from the windows might affect your big screen.

Seating

If you are buying a two-section projection TV, you'll want to be sure all the seating is behind or to the side of the projector. Nothing can interfere with the beam reaching the screen. You can use the projector as a coffee table or an end table and still have a direct shot at the screen.

Care of the Screen

While not as delicate as in the past, big screens should be treated with tender-loving care. Your manual and your dealer should provide instructions on what methods can be used to dust or clean these screens. If Aunt Lucy spills her eggnog on your screen, you'll need to know what, if anything, can be done (for the screen, that is—Aunt Lucy is another problem).

The Doctor Will See You Now

Dr. Knotts's home was beautiful, and he had invested in some fairly involved equipment. The man hadn't a clue as to how to set it up, much less run it or have fun with it.

We got it all set up properly, and he was beginning to catch on to some of the functions when his wife came home. She was cynical: "Well, can you run it yet?" His hands began to tremble, and then he dropped a screw inside the machine that took us ten minutes to retrieve. We went over how to operate the machine a few more times and he seemed to be getting it—but still, the hands shook.

A few days later I saw his picture in the paper. He was an award-winning brain surgeon.

I hope his wife never calls him at work.

Lesson 12

Did You Hear That? Using Your Stereo and VCR Together

How would you like to wear your videos like a second skin? You can wrap yourself in a louder, more stereophonic cinematic experience, all in the privacy of your own home, just by hooking your TV and VCR to your stereo amplifier/receiver. With some of the newer amplifiers, you can even bring on the whole theatrical Dolby Surround Sound experience, just like a fever dream.

If you have a stereo VCR, you can enjoy your movies and television shows in actual stereo, and you can also use your VCR to hook your stereo system into your cable (absolutely free!) This will greatly improve your radio's reception and maximize the number of stations you receive. With the FM antenna attached to cable, you'll be receiving the signals from movie soundtracks plus about twice as many FM stations—everything sent out by the cable transmitters. Talk about command performances. You will be the master, if not the universe, at least your own media system.

Two Ears Are Better Than One   You must have a stereo VCR in order to hook up your VCR to your stereo. It is not necessary to have a stereo TV. If you have a stereo TV but you don't have a stereo VCR, you won't get to hear your movies in stereo.

A Brief Look at the Amplifier/Receiver's Capabilities

Your sound system's amplifier and receiver work together as the brains of your stereo system, much the way the VCR is becoming the brains behind your television system. The amplifier is Big Brother, the power source for your stereo; it is most often, though not always, contained within your receiver. The receiver is your stereo's tuner (radio) and may also control the compact disc, tape deck, and phono outputs. If your amplifier is a separate unit, you can ignore it for the purposes of this lesson.

Hooking Up the FM Transmission Available from the Cable to Your Amplifier/Receiver

Most people don't realize that FM radio channels come through their cable television transmission cable. These channels include the audio broadcasted from cable television. Those in the know usually get the cable company to make the attachment to the antenna lead on their FM radio. This leads to another monthly charge which is completely avoidable. You can make this attachment yourself with the same ease with which Ben Franklin invented the lightning rod.

You'll need the following:

- ☞ amplifier/receiver

- ☞ splitter

- ☞ matching transformer

☛ 3 coaxial cables

☛ VCR

☛ TV

Follow these steps:

1. Attach the splitter to the cable system coming into the house (see Figure 12.1).

2. Attach one part of the splitter to your cable box or cable-ready VCR, which is attached to your TV the usual way.

3. Screw a coaxial cable into the other side of the splitter. Put a matching transformer's cable terminal onto this cable.

4. The remaining part of the matching transformer will have two horseshoe type terminals, which attach to the back of the amplifier/receiver FM radio antenna input.

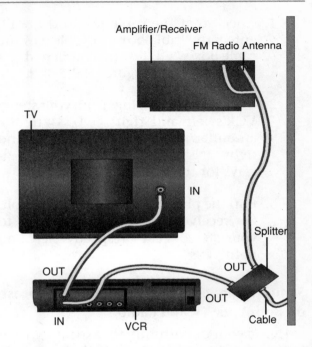

Figure 12.1. *Getting FM transmission from your cable.*

Hooking Up the Cable to Your VCR and Amplifier/Receiver

The following instructions work only for stereo VCRs.

1. Check that the cable leaves the wall, enters the cable box's "IN," leaves the cable box's "OUT," and is attached to a VCR's "IN" (see Figure 12.2).

2. Now, run phono plugs from your stereo VCR's left and right "OUTs" to the amplifier/receiver's respective left and right "INs". The red phono plug is always for the right.

3. Run the phono plugs from your amplifier/receiver's left and right "OUTs" to your stereo VCR's respective left and right "INs".

Simulcasting: Listening to a Cable Broadcast on Both Your TV and Radio

Here's your opportunity to take rather than give to the cable company that regularly drains your wallet. It's not silent revenge, it's stereo. Ask your cable company for a list of FM stations and their location on your radio's FM dial. The cable company probably rebroadcasts the radio stations at different radio frequencies. Your cable company also has a list of soundtracks that are available in stereo. Have them send you this list too, but don't let them come out to help you install this, since you've just done that.

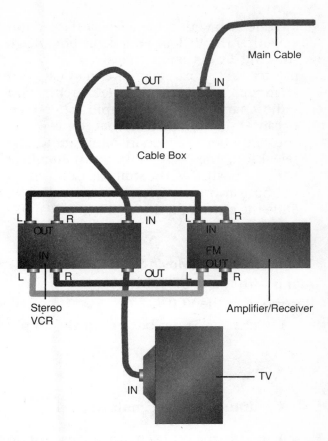

Main Cable

OUT   IN

Cable Box

L   R   IN   L   R

OUT   IN   FM
             OUT
IN   OUT
L   R   L   R

Stereo
VCR

Amplifier/Receiver

IN   TV

Figure 12.2. *Hooking up the cable to your VCR and amplifier/receiver.*

Tune into your cable television selection via either the VCR or your cable box. Make sure the TV set is on channel 3. If you're using a cable box, make sure the VCR is on channel 3, too. Tune into the matching FM radio channel on your amplifier/receiver. Because you want to hear what comes out of the amplifier/receiver in addition to the television, the VCR must be in *simulcast mode* (you will find the simulcast/2nd channel button on the front of a stereo VCR). Slide the button on the VCR box to "simulcast."

To Record Stereo Movie Soundtracks Along with the Cable Movie Being Recorded on the VCR

1. Push the Tuner button on the amplifier/receiver.

2. Choose "FM."

3. Put the VCR on simulcast mode.

4. Locate the cable channel you want on the FM dial by referring to your listing from the cable company.

5. Use the VCR recording instructions from Lesson 8. Follow the usual recording procedure for your amplifier/receiver.

Speaking in Tons: Adding More Speakers

Don't just think about putting speakers in every room. Do it. Most amplifier/receiver models accommodate an A and B speaker system. That is, two speakers left and right for "A" and two speakers left and right for "B," a total of four speakers.

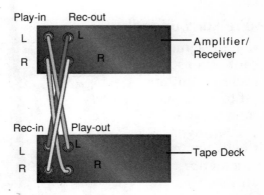

Figure 12.3. *Hooking up the cable to your VCR and amplifier/receiver.*

You can add a speaker control center, available at an electronics supply store for about $30.00, to make the sound from your FM, CD, tape deck, TV, and VCR fly throughout your house.

This small unit drives sets of speakers, which you can turn on or off as you please. You can have sound in the living room, but not in the bedroom. Sound on the patio, but not in the kitchen. Or sound in all three rooms. Connect the pairs of speakers from your amplifier/receiver (the "A" and "B" terminals) to the speaker control center.

You're Surrounded!

If your significant other still prefers hauling off to a theater mob scene to cocooning in the intimate cinematic atmosphere you've cooked up at home, maybe it's time to resort to surround sound.

The surround sound system is based upon the Dolby Pro Logic Surround Decoder (brought to you by the same guy that invented Dolby Noise Reduction, a feature now standard on most tape decks). By utilizing no less than five speakers, at least three stereo channels, and some hocus pocus called the adjusted delay time, the surround sound system puts your ears right in the middle of the action on screen. If you are watching a movie and there is a helicopter coming over a hill, you can hear it thwacking from behind and over you; you may even think it's going to land on you. Surround sound gives you the most realistic sound that the video or motion-picture people can presently muster. Video cassettes that have Dolby stereo have an extra sound track that you will only be able to hear if you have the surround-sound feature.

You can buy amplifier/receivers with the surround-sound capability built in, which will set you back an additional $100–$200 depending on the brand and the quality of the components. In my opinion, the price is well worth the improvement in quality. All you need to do is plug all of the speakers into the back of your amplifier/receiver and lounge back into the divan with your mate.

However, if you're in the mood to skimp, or you want to adapt the amplifier/receiver you already have, you can jury-rig pseudo surround sound with an adapter called the Surround Sound Decoder. Although less expensive than surround sound, the decoder takes considerable patience to install.

There are variations to this setup, but the basic concept follows: The adapter is connected to two rear (live) speakers. This creates the extra sound track that we've been discussing. You then connect a third speaker to the adapter which is placed in front. The amplifier/receiver feeds the adapter, which in turn feeds the three speakers. The two regular front speakers (left and right) operate from your amplifier/receiver as always. See Figure 12.3 for an example of a surround-sound speaker system.

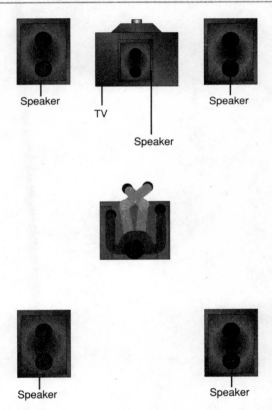

Figure 12.4. *Surround yourself with sound.*

Lesson 13

Laser Disc Players

It's Not a Frisbee, It's the Future

For deeper color saturation, sharper definition and noise-free pictures, you can't beat
laser technology. Laser disc players run circles
around VCRs. Weigh the visual and aural
quality of a tape against that of a disc and
you'll agree—the tape looks and sounds like
mush by comparison. The improvement is
radical—up to 20–25% better.

So, if these gadgets are so great, why don't
we all own one? We've been hearing about
laser disc players for over a decade. Pioneer
introduced the first optical videodisc player
to North America in 1980. But videotape
technology was already entrenched. Laser
disc players are considerably more expensive, they lack a disc rental market and—the
biggie—they don't record.

So, other than picture and sound quality,
what's the big deal? With fewer and tougher
parts, laser discs don't get dog-eared with
repeated use. Laser disc players can move
from track to track like greased lightning.
They can be programmed to play selected
tracks of a program in any order.

However, prices are lower by more than half in the last few years. 1992 sales were 23 percent higher than 1991. Part of this increase is attributable to "combi-players," which play audio compact discs too. Mail-order clubs and retailers sell ordinary versions of movies for $20 to $30 and specialty discs for over $100. The players cost from $300 to $700 and up.

Trouble is, when investing in laser technology, you're not just investing in the box. You need a great monitor/tuner, the sound processor, multiple speakers, and a lot of cables.

And as long as you're going hog-wild anyway, you probably need bells and whistles. A few follow:

- ☛ Digital time-base corrector, for reducing picture jitter.

- ☛ Three-line digital comb filter, for sharpening color edges.

- ☛ Digital dropout compensator, for minimizing imperfections on dirty or scratched discs.

- ☛ S-video jack, for delivering color and brightness information separately.

☛ Shuttle ring on remote, for scanning discs at various speeds.

☛ Karaoke machine, for feigning to be Madonna or Batman.

☛ Auto-reversing transport mechanism, for flipping the disc automatically.

☛ Optional "lights-out" on the front panel.

☛ Inner jog-dial, for moving the picture one frame at a time, forward or backward, while the outer dial scans both directions.

☛ CD changer (on combis only), for playing several CDs (but not laser discs) without pause.

Inherently, laser discs are less expensive to produce because the actual technology is more straightforward—stamp 'em out and cover them with a protective plastic coating. This isn't always true in practice, because they are not produced in the same volume as videotape cassettes. Unfortunately, the machinery required to record on laser discs is still prohibitive, like $26,000-worth of prohibitive. Laser discs have a way to go before they really start to impinge on the VCR market.

Hooking Up the Laser Disc Player

You have a number of possible ways to hook up your laser disc player to your video system. Here are three.

Most disc players are equipped to connect directly to the newer stereo TVs with either phono plugs or RF connectors. For maximum stereo effect, use phono plugs (Figure 13.1).

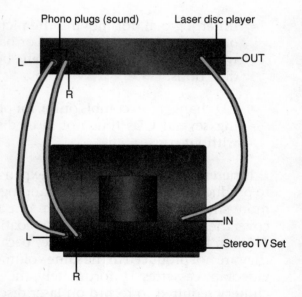

Figure 13.1 *Connecting a laser disc player to a stereo TV.*

Now let's add a little complexity. Figure 13.2 shows a hookup that links the laser disc player to a TV-and-VCR system through an A-B switch box. On A of the A-B switch, you'll get regular cable programs. On B, you'll get the laser disc playback. Set the VCR on 3, the TV on channel 3, turn on the laser disc, and voilà! (If you have an amp/rec, jack into AUX with phono plugs, and your laser disc sound will come through in wonderful stereo.)

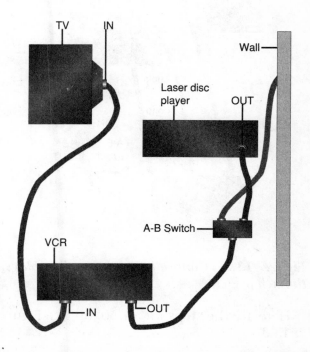

Figure 13.2 *Connecting a laser disc player to a TV-VCR system with an A-B switch box.*

If you hook up your laser disc player with both picture and sound going through the VCR, you can make a copy of the laser disc on tape (See Figure 13.3).

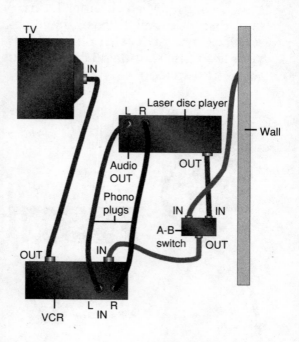

Figure 13.3 Connecting a laser disc player through a VCR.

Here are the steps for a hookup like Figure 13.3:

1. Cable OUT of wall into A of A-B switch.

2. Cable OUT of laser disc player into B of A-B switch.

3. Cable OUT of A-B switch into VCR.

4. Cable OUT of VCR into TV.

5. Phono plugs L and R OUT to L and R IN on VCR.

On A of A-B switch, straight cable information moves through the VCR into the TV.On B of A-B switch, information from the laser disc player moves through the VCR into the TV.

Lesson 14

Remote Control: Why Americans Need Fitness Centers

Remotes have made relaxation not just restful but slothful. In theory anyway, modifications to your channel selection, volume and recording expend few calories and free up your body to eat chips and drink brew. Legs are reduced to mere props, keeping you from sliding off the couch. Not to wax on and on, but remotes impart a wierd power to whomever wields them. Many people go into a frenzy of channel switching. It sometimes seems they are sitting in front of the tube not to watch television, but to switch channels. For most people, remotes are now a crucial part of the television experience.

No one knows exactly how this happened, but originally, the remote was a piece of wire, with a couple of slide switches, all attached to the VCR or TV itself. It was used to stop the machines, to start them, and occasionally to change the channels with ultra sound. However, people kept tripping over the remote cord, sometimes injuring themselves and often pulling it out of the device. In order to alleviate this problem, our Japanese friends came up with a way to have infared light carry information from the remote to the TV or VCR.

Suddenly, these super-capable remotes multiplied like bacteria, but all for different machines. Remotes for every conceivable household function appeared from the TV set to the VCR, from the sound department for tape decks and amplifiers/receivers to the garage door. Every home accrued its own pile of remotes, unsightly, confusing, incompatible, and just plain controversial. Everyone has been bellyaching for some way to fully operate equipment with one remote.

Remotely "Universal"

Thus was developed a device known as the *universal remote,* sometimes known by other names (not all of them printable here). The universal remote attempts to transfer most of the controls to one cordless remote. The universal remote means that you have only one remote to lose in the depths of your couch cushions, as opposed to the six you used to have to dig around for. The universal remote has had a modicum of success. However, it is another expenditure (somewhere in the neighborhood of fifty-plus dollars), and it hasn't always been that functionally accurate. It continues to have a transfer problem. You'll find that certain VCR brands' remotes are not compatible with each other for transfer, sending you once again up off the couch. It's enough to turn couch potatoes to mash potatoes.

Also, there are various controls such as channel change, index, and so on that still require the use of both remotes. There was a dispute about this, so the 2,583 companies listed the names of their competitors in order to help us understand which VCRs and TVs would be most compatible in order to have a single remote to handle most of the controls.

Another problem with the universal remote is that no one really wants to spend the time to decipher the four thousand buttons on the front. Technology still has a way to go before "push-button convenience" is truly convenient. Stay tuned.

A Remote That Can Read the Newspaper—VCRPlus

VCR Plus (bought for about $50), which I touched on in Lesson 8, is perhaps the most significant advance in the remote field.

Think for a moment; practically everyone has problems programming their VCRs. VCRPlus has a code number arrangement that corresponds to the code published in *TV Guide* and many newspapers. When you enter those code numbers on the VCRPlus, your VCR will record the program, whether daily, weekly, monthly, one time, four times a day—you name it. Seems fantastic, and it is.

The biggest advantage I see to VCRPlus over any other system that you've encountered so far (and there are more encounterable) is that you will be able to program your cable box from your control box, whether it has pay channels or not. Those channels will change and be automatically programmed just like the channels on your VCR. This hasn't been possible before now. Although it works, we don't see this being done too often, perhaps because in order to do it, the original setup becomes a little bit complicated. Well, let's make that "a lot complicated." The VCRPlus is the best so far—but inevitably, there is still a problem. It's a bear to set up. The VCRPlus has a section in the instruction book referring to cable box. In setting up a pay channel, to be recorded at 7:30, use the VCRPlus code numbers. I have found this to be quite workable in recording not one but several programs. The control box is necessary in the hookup as is the VCR, cable box and TV. Wouldn't you know it?

Caveat Emptor Some VCRs, those which don't use infrared signals for remotes, cannot use VCRPlus at all. Make sure to ask about this before you invest in a VCRPlus system.

Multiple Remotes: the Five-Cent Solution Don't invest in a universal remote or VCRPlus. Buy some double-stick, foam-backed tape. Put a couple of strips on the underside of the TV remote. Line up the VCR remote, strip the paper off the tape, and press them together—voila, you've done it. Nothing to it. You now have just one remote. You may even want to try Velcro.

Setting Up the VCRPlus System

Okay, so you have a VCRPlus system and you want to keep it. While it is more convenient than the usual programming methods, there can be problems setting it up. When you enter the plus code numbers, you can verify the program information you have punched in, but the settings of the code numbers don't always agree with those of your cable or the regular antenna numbers in your area. So you have to make substitutions. There is a supplement folder included with the VCRPlus. This is a must read—providing more information than you need. It also describes a test setup, which runs your VCRPlus for a short time to make sure it is working correctly. Why ask why? Just do it! And all this is just the initial setup. If things become too frustrating, call the VCRPlus 800 number.

You May Already Have One   VCRPlus can be bought separately or imbedded in many new models of VCRs. How much more costly is a whole-ball-of-wax VCR with VCRPlus? Not too much, maybe thirty dollars.

Monkey Business Many who have purchased the additional VCRPlus discover that after monkeying around with the VCRPlus setup, they really seem to have mastered conventional programming on their VCRs anyway, just from learning to use the VCRPlus device correctly. So get the fifty bucks back and go out for Chinese with the whole family—and leave a big tip. Oh yes, record your shows while you're out to dinner.

Sit Up! Beg! Roll Over!: The VCR Voice-Programmer

For the terminally nonmechanical consumer, there is the VCR Voice-Programmer. All you have to do is to speak into it, and all your programming desires are taken care of. If you can talk, they say you can program your VCR. You can scoot through the commercials as you have done with your regular VCR remote. Go backward, forward, fast forward, and reverse. Also, you can change channels just by saying the channel number. But be careful when you use numbers in conversation!

The VCR Voice-Programmer is not being sold in stores, per se. Certain stores are market testing, but basically this item is being sold by mail order only. Look for VCR Voice-Programmers being built into some television sets by one or two rather large companies in the near future. Right now, the cost is somewhere in the neighborhood of $140.00 to $170.00.

However, the VCR Voice-Programmer is very sophisticated. Suddenly, just like on "Star Trek: The Next Generation," you're talking to a machine and it actually listens. Your not pushing buttons as much. You have time to drink your coffee or wave at the cute new neighbor across the street.

This voice-programmed remote is the wave of the future. Add HDTV (stands for high definition TV) which features 1125 lines of resolution (TV's now have 525) and all the other innovations, and the future seems truly incredible.

Setting Up the VCR Voice-Programmer

As with the VCRPlus, there can be problems with the setup. Many of the problems with voice programmer setup are essentially traceable to a lack of understanding of the basic VCR. Again, I must let you know that you should be able to program your VCR as the manufacturer intended no matter what. Best check your VCR programming setup. Push the buttons, so you know you can do it.

Lesson 15

Camcorders and Editing

Can I Delete the Part Where I Split My Pants Open?

Home movies have always been a great source of both embarrassment and pleasure. What was hokey and flickery in the Brownie movie camera days is now so superbly produced that Hollywood is exploiting amateur videos nationally on home-video TV shows. VCR technology has made customizing home movies a snap. With an 8-millimeter camcorder glued to your socket, you become your own Speilberg, your own "Frontline." Lug it with you to parties so you can embarrass and even blackmail family and friends who are in the video. And later, using your VCR, you can edit out all of the scenes that might embarrass *you*.

You can either play the tape on your VCR through the camcorder or transfer your movies from your eight millimeter camcorder tape onto a VHS tape for the family video library. While doing this you can edit out those humiliations and expunge dull sections of the video, like when you forgot you were recording and you recorded fifteen minutes of the car door. You may even want to put your "shoots" together and do something a bit creative, like add music or narration.

Edit is a scary word when it comes to VCRs and camcorders. But it's not as tough as it sounds. To make a transfer from a camcorder to a VCR, you essentially play what you've recorded on the camcorder into a VCR which is on channel 3. Follow these steps:

1. Put your VCR on channel 3.

2. Make the connection from the camcorder "RF OUT" to the VCR input, replacing the cable or antenna. Better yet, if you have an A/B switch, the camcorder "OUT" can go into the "A" of an A/B switch, the cable goes into "B," and the third connection is attached to the VCR input. This way you can continue to use the VCR in the usual manner without having to undo cables each time.

When you switch to "B" you have the regular cable/antenna input. When you switch to "A" (providing your camcorder is attached) you will see what's on your camcorder. See Figure 15.1.

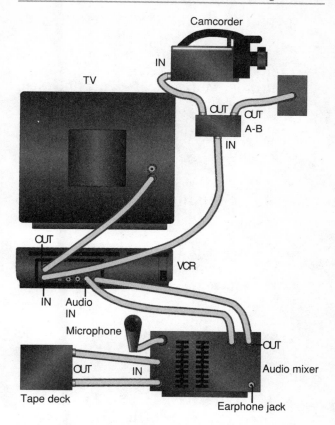

Figure 15.1. Hooking up the camcorder and VCR.

Editing with the Camcorder VCR Hookup

1. Tune both the VCR and the TV to channel 3.

2. Write down the order of your scenes.

3. Use the counter/reset/memory function on your VCR. If your scenes aren't
   in order, you can go back and find them
   more easily.

4. For the recording, use a fresh T120 tape.
   Record at the SP speed.

5. When you reach the end of the first
   scene, push the Pause button on the
   VCR.

6. Locate scene 2 by viewing the material
   on the camcorder and push Pause on
   the camcorder. (Both machines are now
   on Pause.)

7. Now take both machines off Pause.
   When scene 2 is over, put the VCR on
   Pause.

8. Repeat this process until all scenes have
   been transferred to the T120 VCR tape.
   You'll get the rhythm of it after a bit of
   practice.

Tip

Taking a Break Already? If you take a break, push the counter on the VCR before hitting the Stop button. Since the tape creeps after stopping, you will be able to rewind to the exact number. Stop the camcorder, too.

Tip

Fleshing out Special Effects In this normal editing method without special equipment you can't put in fancy effects, such as dissolves and wipes while editing. Plan your fades (in and out) ahead of time, before shooting. You still can do interesting things with the camera.

Adding Voice and Music

Now add music and narration or dialogue.

You'll need the following:

☞ An inexpensive ($25.00 to $30.00) audio mixer from your electronic store

☛ microphone

☛ earphones

Follow these steps:

1. Attach the microphone and earphones to the appropriate jacks on the back of the mixer (see Figure 15.1).

2. Bring the phono plugs out of left and right outputs of the mixer and plug them into the left and right audio inputs of your VCR.

3. If the VCR is not stereo, use a Y connector to join the left and right outputs of the mixer into one phono plug inserted into VCR input. Use all phono plugs, not coaxial-cable connectors.

4. Feed music out of a tapedeck.

5. Choose your background music and have your narration ready—scene by scene.

6. Move the slide switches on your mixer up and down for music and narration mix.

7. VCRs have a switch to simulcast which will allow you to record in stereo without distributing or erasing or changing your picture.

8. Place your edited tape in the VCR. Before you begin recording, you will probably want to take a few practice runs with your narration and music. Put your VCR in simulcast position by moving the little switch button on the box to "simulcast." This way, when you do actually record, you will be working off both the audio mixer and the VCR. Press Play.

9. Begin your narration and music. In this way you will hear the total mix of the original voice recording plus your added music and narration. You will not be erasing any audio, so feel free to practice as much as you like before actually mixing.

10. Now add narration and music in simulcast mode with the VCR on Record. Keep an eye on the counter so if you make a mistake in adding this audio track, you can rewind to the place on the counter where you made the error, and then pick up the narration or music from there.

Talking About Nothing   Warning! Never record using the tuner mode (normal recording mode), since that will erase all audio and video on the tape. If you do accidentally do this, all is not totally lost. You still have your camcorder copy but you will have to re-edit.

Stereo VCRs are preferable for editing because you have a second channel on which you can put your narration/music mix. Obviously, mono VCRs can handle only one recorded segment at a time.

You can record your music and narration between dialogue scenes. This can work out quite well as long as you do not overlap your music/narration over the original recording.

Photo CD Player, Real and Simulated

Kodak has come out with a photo CD player. The unit puts pictures on TV by converting snapshots (through Kodak processing) to compact discs. These can be played like audio or video discs into their CD player and the picture quality is excellent. But you don't have to buy the extra player and lock into Kodak.

I've had very good luck using the macro feature on my video camera (and camcorder) to put favorite photos on tape. Stack about ten to fifteen pictures at a time (in some sort of order, naturally) and lean them at a slight backward angle against a box or anything that won't move around on you. An easel or a drafting table is perfect. Focus in with your camera; you want good light but no glare. You don't want to see the edges of the pictures, so fill the screen. A tripod will keep things steady. Leave each picture for about five seconds. Use a knife to slide behind the photo and flip it forward to show the next photo. It really is a nice way to put your trip on tape. Throw some music playing in the background and narrate as you go.

Also, when you opt for your camcorder over the Photo CD player to record pictures, for added quality use special effects such as zoom or fade, and add dialogue or sound.

Tip

He Who Dies with the Most Toys . . .
Phillips (the inventor of the camcorder and the compact disc) has further pushed the technology envelope with a new device called CD-I, the "Imagination Machine." Not only will this unit play your CD snapshots, but it will also play Phillips' entire line of software, including Compton's CD Interactive Encyclopedia, a 26-volume encyclopedia on a single compact disc. If you're going to drop the extra cash for the photo CD player, you might want to consider this one.

Appendix

Accessories

As you hook up your VCR to different electronic equipment, you may need accessories and tools to accomplish your goals. This appendix shows the accessories you may need, with a short description of each.

Figure A.1. *Round coaxial cable. A solid center conductor surrounded by a heavy plastic called the dielectric. Around this is a mesh of braid that acts as a second conductor and shield against external interference. The entire cable is insulated*

continues

with black plastic. This type of cable is used by telephone companies, cable companies, and by you. It gives excellent reception because it is protected. Sometimes it is called "RF cable"; RF means "radio frequency." It has within it two axes, that accommodate both the VHF and UHF input bands. Most often, the cable you buy has one "female" end (with a needle hole) and the other "male" (with a needle).

Figure A.2. *A UHF/VHF/FM matching transformer. Flat wire, coated with plastic with two separate wires in horseshoe-shaped finishes.*

Figure A.3. *A push-on matching transformer. Use for transforming a double-tipped flat wire into*

a round coaxial cable finish. This unit can be pushed on the input of the VCR.

Figure A.4. *A signal splitter. Use for transforming a round coaxial cable into separate UHF and VHF bands, the UHF with a round coaxial cable finish and the VHF with two screw-type finishes.*

Figure A.5. *A signal combiner/decombiner. Use for combining separate UHF and VHF input bands and decombining combined UHF and VHF input bands.*

Figure A.6. *An A-B switch. Receives two signals, either of which can be sent to a single component.*

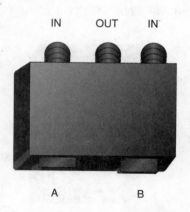

Figure A.7. *A pushbutton deluxe A-B switch. This is the best. You can stack them if you are using more than one in a setup (using foam-backed double-stick tape) and all the cables come out from the back for a neater appearance.*

Figure A.8. *An RF connector with a ring attachment. This must be attached to either end of a standard RG59U coaxial cable. To attach connector to cable, the cable must be stripped, revealing a center pin (a wire about 1/2 inch). In turn, push the connector over the pin, crimp the attached ring to the cable, and cut off the center pin nearly flush. The pin should protrude slightly for best contact. Special tools can be purchased for this process if desired.*

Figure A.9. *An RCA phono plug. This type of plug with a cord attached is inserted into the VCR out jack (or jacks) usually found in the rear of VCRs. The line(s) coming from these plugs are inserted into the left and right phono jacks in the rear of the amplifier-receiver, normally marked VCR or AUX. This allows sound to be sent from your VCR into your amplifier/receiver and will enable you to hear improved sound coming from the speakers.*

Figure A.10. *Rabbit ears. Two telescoping wands that stick out of a single housing and are used indoors as an antenna to catch television signals.*

Figure A.11. *Antenna rotor. If your antenna is not receiving clear reception, enhance its performance*

*by attaching an electronic antenna rotor. This will
automatically rotate the outdoor antenna toward
the desired signal when you turn the dial to the
chosen channel on the TV.*

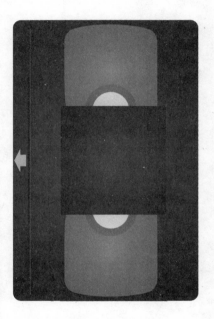

Figure A.12. *T120 video tape in a plastic cassette. T120 means two hours (120 minutes) at
SP (Standard Play), four hours at LP (Long Play),
and six hours at EP or SLP (Extended Play or Super
Long Play).*

Glossary

A-B switch   A two-way switch that is used to divert between two incoming signals, which can be divided by A or B.

antenna   A receiver of signals sent through the air by a transmitter.

attenuator   A device which reduces signal power. The opposite of a booster.

audio mixer   Mixes music, narration, and sound effects necessary to complete the sound portion of your video production... incoming signals

beta   The first widely used VCR format.

booster   A device which amplifies audio and video signal. The opposite of an attenuator.

cable box   Also known as cable converter, a cable box contains a tuner allowing you to receive all cable channels from the cable company.

cable-ready TV   A TV set capable of receiving all or most of the channels being offered by a cable company.

camcorder A VCR and video camera combined.

CD Compact disc (a laser recording).

CD player A device which plays compact discs.

coax Short for *coaxial cable*. Round cable with a wire core (the conductor), a layer of plastic, braided shielding wire and an outer layer of rubber like plastic. Used for connecting video equipment.

control box Also known as switcher and/or selector. Simplifies hook-up procedures with respect to inputs and outputs of the various components in most video systems.

convergence To clarify a color TV picture by bringing the colors together into a white line. This can be done by consumers only on projection TV sets.

copy guard A means of preventing you from copying a videotape on your VCR.

crimper A tool designed to fasten an RF end to coaxial cable.

db (decibel) A unit of measurement used to express the strength of electric or acoustic signals.

Dolby A noise reduction system. Removes hiss, background noise, and so on.

eject A function of the VCR which triggers the removal of a cassette.

EP Extended play. The slowest speed on a VHS VCR.

F connectors RF connectors. These connect the RF inputs and outputs and coaxial cable.

focus When a projected beam or beams of light carrying visual information reaches a flat surface and can be clearly seen.

graphic equalizer (EQ) A device which controls various sections of the audio band.

HDTV High-definition TV.

head The electromagnetic piece of hardware used to convert signals on tape to either audio or video images. All recorders have heads.

hologram A three-dimensional picture using laser beams without the aid of a camera.

indexing A VCR system of numerically marking information for later reference.

infrared A light sensor used in VCR and TV remote-control units. It's a simple circuit that employs three parts: a photo transistor, an LED (light-emitting diode), and a resistor.

input The cable connector for audio and video equipment.

jack A female plug connector. *See also* input.

jacks More than one cable (phono plug) connector in audio and video equipment.

laser videodisc system A video system which uses a coherent light source—a laser beam—for both recording and playback. A totally optical system with no mechanical contact with the videodisc itself.

LP Long play. In VHS, four-hour mode.

master The original recording from which all copies will be made.

matching transformer Matches signal strength between two cables or devices.

output Cable connector for audio and video equipment.

oxide The metallic compound coated onto the base film (the actual "tape"), which can be magnetized to encode and then reproduce a given electronic signal.

pause A function of the VCR that holds pictures in the still mode.

phono plug Also called RCA phono plug. A "push-in" male connector to be used with a female jack input.

photo CD player The Photo CD player allows you to view photographs on a remote-control disc player. Some models also allow you to use this player for audio compact discs.

preset Part of a system used on some older VCR tuners to aid you in manually tuning channels.

Pro Logic Pro Logic amplifier/receivers receive a high beam of channel separations for pinpoint signal location. When correctly set up, you climb into the same atmosphere with the on-screen performer. Crowds mumble, symphonic orchestras resound all around you. If the hero throws a punch—you just might duck.

projection TV A television using (usually) 3 projection beams (blue, green and red), which are similar to TV tubes. These beams carry the same information as seen on color TV sets, but are projected and converged to a focal point on front or rear screens to a much larger size.

rabbit ears An indoor antenna which pulls in signals from a transmitter.

reverb Electronically produced echo.

RF connector *See* F connector.

selector box *See* control box.

shielding Conducting material around (but insulated from) the electrical conductor.

signal combiner A device used for antenna reception on a VCR when antenna must combine VHF and VHF signals. Some VCRs have only a combined signal input.

signal decombiner A device used for antenna reception when VHF and UHF signals have been combined prior to reaching the VCR. For most VCRs these signals would have to be separated again and attached to UHF and VHF terminals.

simulcast A broadcast both seen on television and heard on radio. Cable companies broadcast simulcasts on the FM radio band.

splitter A device allowing one signal to be sent equally two ways at the same time to video equipment.

still Pause mode on a VCR.

strength meter A device which shows how many DBs (decibels) you are receiving from the cable company. By law you must have 0 to 5 DBs.

Surround Sound A sound option for use with audio, TV and VCRs that uses specifically encoded rear channel sounds to create dynamic effects.

timer A device used to delay recording until a prescribed time and then to end that function at another predetermined time.

tracking The angle and method in which the tape passes the heads.

tracking control Something to check before you take back your rented tape saying "it's no good." Changes the tracking timing on the VCR to accommodate prerecorded material from another VCR with different timing.

UHF Ultra-high frequency TV signals; channels 14–83.

VCR An acronym for Video Cassette Recorder.

VHF Very high frequency TV signals; channels 2–13.

VHS An acronym for Video Home System.

VL Very low frequency signals; used for radio transmissions, and (on first- and second-generation VCRs) channels 2–6.

VTR An acronym for Video Tape Recorder.

Y connector A device which takes two signals and equally combines them for use on non-stereo VCR outputs so that sound will be evenly distributed from the amplifier/receiver to the speakers.

Index

U-V

W-Z

Other
Idiot-Proof
Books from
Alpha!

If you enjoyed this Complete Idiot's Pocket Guide, then you may want to check out the rest!

Complete Idiot's Pocket Guides

Cheaper Than Therapy!

Complete Idiot's Guides

Learn everything you need to know about computers from our best-selling series!

The Complete Idiot's Guide to Windows
ISBN: 1-56761-175-3
Softbound, $14.95 USA

The Complete Idiot's Guide to DOS
ISBN: 1-56761-169-9
Softbound, $14.95 USA

The Complete Idiot's Guide to PCs
ISBN: 1-56761-168-0
Softbound, $14.95 USA

The Complete Idiot's Guide to Word for Windows
ISBN: 1-56761-174-5
Softbound, $14.95 USA

The Complete Idiot's Guide to WordPerfect
ISBN: 1-56761-187-7
Softbound, $14.95 USA

The Complete Idiot's Guide to Computer Terms
ISBN: 1-56761-266-0
Softbound, $9.95 USA

The Complete Idiot's Guide to 1-2-3
ISBN: 1-56761-285-7
Softbound, $14.95 USA

The Complete Idiot's Guide to VCRs
ISBN: 1-56761-294-6
Softbound, $9.95 USA

If you can't find these books at your local computer book retailer, call this toll-free number for more information! 1-800-428-5331